THE Wealthy CODE

What the Wealthy Know About Money That Most People Will Never Know!

GEORGE ANTONE

WEALTHCLASSES PUBLISHING
www.WealthclassesPublishing.com

The Wealthy Code
By George Antone
www.TheWealthyCodeBook.com

FIRST EDITION

Printed in the United States of America

Book design by TLC Graphics, *www.TLCGraphics.com*
Cover by Monica Thomas / Interior by Erin Stark
Cover photo: ©*iStockphoto.com/JLGutierrez*

Certain events in this book, although based on a true story, have been fictionalized
for educational content and impact.

Rich Dad Poor Dad, The Cashflow Quadrant, and CASHFLOW® are the registered
trademarks of CASHFLOW Technologies, Inc.

ISBN: 098270450X

This publication is designed to provide information with regard to the subject matter
covered. It is sold with the understanding that the publisher and author are not
engaged in rendering real estate, legal, accounting, tax, or other professional services
and that the publisher and author are not offering such advice in this publication. If
real estate, legal, or other expert assistance is required, the services of a competent
professional should be sought. The publisher and author specifically disclaim any
liability incurred from the use or application of the contents of this book.

I DEDICATE THIS BOOK TO MY FAMILY.

My parents: Emile and Jacqueline. You taught me that
I can achieve anything I believe. That lesson shaped
my life. You have been my greatest inspiration.

My uncles: Antoun, Rene, and Raymond.
You helped me and my brothers in time of need.
You gave us an opportunity very few get. The words
"thank you" just don't say how appreciative we are.

My brothers: Emile and Farid. You have always been
supportive, no matter how crazy my ideas were.

Finally, my wife Clara and our children:
Emile, Amanda, and Christine. Thank you for
being the greatest family anyone could ask for.
You mean the world to me. This is for you.

TABLE OF CONTENTS

ACKNOWLEDGEMENTS

"If I have seen further than others,
it is by standing upon the shoulders of Giants."

SIR ISAAC NEWTON WROTE THOSE WORDS IN 1676. THEY ALSO APPLY TO me today. Many people before me have written books that open our eyes and challenge our beliefs. These authors change people's lives. I am grateful to them.

I also want to recognize those I work with at WealthClasses.com for always pushing me to do better. Likewise, thanks to my many business partners who have pointed me in the right direction: Gary Boomershine, Haider Nazar, and Phong Dang — you guys absolutely rock! Stephanie May — I would not be where I am without your help. Mark Peters — you are simply an amazing human being. John Taylor — you definitely rock! Anthony Chara — thank you for being the most trustworthy person I know, at least in Colorado! Swanee Heidberg — thank you for allowing me to hassle you with this book and everything else I am working on. Mami Yamajo — I cannot do anything without you either. Tim McGilberry — thanks for believing in us. The rest of the WealthClasses crew — it is a pleasure to work with all of you. Vadim — welcome aboard. Phil Brothers — hang in there, buddy. Jim Britt — it's great working with you. My mentor who prefers not to be mentioned — you are an inspiration; I have learned a lot from you. My in-laws — thank you for all that you do. My students — you have made me want to excel and be the best I can be. Thank you.

This book would not have been possible without Bette Daoust, Tom and Tamara Dever, and everyone else at TLC Graphics. Thank you so much.

FOREWORD

IF YOU'RE WORKING HARDER AND HARDER JUST TO MAKE ENDS MEET, then it could be that you're making one or more of the mistakes made by most people who search for a better financial future.

The one element the wealthy of the world have in common is how easy it was for them to succeed financially when they finally understood how the moneymaking system works.

The problem is, this is training *you* never received in high school, college, or on the job. Until now, only the lucky few had a family member or close friend who shared these wealth-building insights, or perhaps the lucky ones simply stumbled upon them by trial and error. Not a good way to plan your financial future.

I know the author of this book, George Antone. I've seen him work. I know the kind of results he produces for those who attend his wealth-building classes. Right now, you hold in your hands an unprecedented opportunity to tap into some proprietary wealth-building concepts and strategies from one of today's brightest wealth masters. If you apply this information, it could set you free financially.

George has been empowering middle-income individuals with a desire for more, to become wealthy — and even financially successful people to become super wealthy — by making the right investments at the right time.

Now, for the first time ever, George is offering you what he teaches at his wealth-building events. Not only are you going to receive some of the secrets of the wealthy, you'll also be inspired by some of the personal stories he shares.

The most amazing thing about wealth is how easy it is to attain once you know the rules of the game and play by those rules. Can you just imagine the peace of mind you'll experience once you have your financial future handled forever?

This book truly delivers! George doesn't pull any punches. You will get direct, action-oriented wealth-building advice that works.

If, however, you are not willing to act on the lessons and strategies in this content-rich book, then my suggestion is — don't buy it.

I have learned from being around wealthy people that the starting point for wealth is having a mentor *and* taking action. So, if you are one of those remarkable individuals who takes responsibility for your life and the results you produce, this book was written just for you, and I urge you to hang on every word.

To be wealthy you have to seize opportunities as they arise. This book is such an opportunity. You were born to be wealthy. Act now!

Jim Britt
Author *Do This. Get Rich!*

PART ONE

Introduction

CHAPTER ONE

Robert Kiyosaki Changed Many Lives

I TURNED ON THE TELEVISION. FINDING NOTHING EXCITING TO WATCH, I started channel surfing. One show piqued my interest: *On The Record with Greta Van Susteren*. Greta was interviewing a man about wealth and how the rich become wealthy. His ideas were very different from those of the mainstream. The man in the interview was Robert Kiyosaki, and the book he was being interviewed about was *Rich Dad Poor Dad*.

Robert Kiyosaki has changed many lives since then — including mine. His books, *Rich Dad Poor Dad* and *The Cashflow Quadrant,* have introduced people to new ways of thinking about becoming wealthy. The books have also challenged traditional notions, such as considering the home you live in a financial asset, becoming rich without first becoming wealthy, and other conventional concepts. In the process Kiyosaki has introduced readers to the ways of the rich, thinking how they think, seeing what they see, and speaking their language.

He gave us the "glasses" of the rich so that we can see things the way they see them. When the media said, "Get out of debt," he said, "Get *into* debt." When the media said, "The greatest investment is your home," he said "The house you live in is a liability." When accountants defined assets and liabilities, he rewrote those definitions and, in the process, opened our eyes.

He first introduced readers to the basics — such as reading income statements and balance sheets — and then he brought them advanced concepts, such as gold vs. the U.S. dollar. In the process, he changed millions of lives.

Some have said that his books lack detail. That, in fact, is the strength and the uniqueness of Kiyosaki's books. He is changing the way his readers think, educating them to think as the rich think.

Those critics say, "Just tell me what I have to do to become wealthy, and I will do it." Kiyosaki's reply is this: You have to first learn to think on your own, and that ability to think comes from a solid financial education. When you begin to think on your own, you are ready to build wealth. This ability is more important than specific, detailed how-to skills; these come *after* you have mastered the thinking process.

Look at it like this: Imagine walking into a bookstore and buying a book titled *How To Build a Home With a Hammer Alone*. You read the book and then spend years trying to perfect that skill. Then along comes a wise, successful man who shares with you a simple approach to achieving your objective without having to do anything the book taught you. A few words from that wise man and you recognize the path you need to take. You also realize that you wasted years of your life walking down the wrong path. You were so focused on mastering a single skill that you missed the big picture.

Robert Kiyosaki's books are the words of wisdom that will open your eyes so that you can finally see the path to your financial goals. He is the wise man telling you to step back and see the big picture.

Don't waste your life going down the wrong road.

Problem Solved

A solid understanding of the lessons in *Rich Dad Poor Dad* is key to the effectiveness of the information in this book. I recommend that you read it.

However, for those of you who desire a more-detailed approach to acquiring wealth, I will address your need. I will continue where Kiyosaki left off. Specifically, I am going to focus on the details you need to know that will make you wealthy.

> ## I will focus on what you need to know to become wealthy.

Wealth is generally defined as "having a large amount of money or property." However, in this book I will use Kiyosaki's definition of having enough passive income to pay for your living expenses, with the emphasis on "passive income."

> ## Being wealthy is having enough passive income to pay for your living expenses.

For example, if your expenses are $5,000 a month and your passive income is $6,000 a month, then you can afford to choose whether or not you continue to work, since your passive income covers your living expenses. You're not necessarily rich, but you are definitely wealthy. This is the definition of wealth I will be using throughout this book.

Kiyosaki teaches that we have to become wealthy before we become rich. Learning that was a big moment for me. Instead of aiming for the $1 million mark, all I had to do was aim for enough passive income to cover my living expenses.

> **Being "rich" is currently defined as having a net worth of at least one million U.S. dollars or of having made at least $200,000 each year for the past two years ($300,000 with spouse, if married) and having the expectation of making the same amount this year.**

Many people pursue wealth without knowing anything about it. They are simply shooting in the dark and hoping riches will fall their way. This seldom happens. Others read Kiyosaki's books, learn his approach, and then turn around and do something completely different.

I don't recommend either approach. The rest of this book will explain why.

Cashflow®: The Game

In Kiyosaki's board game, *Cashflow*®, players learn that to get out of the "Rat Race," you need to first become wealthy. In the *Cashflow*® game the idea is to purchase enough income-producing assets to exceed your everyday living expenses. You can do this by purchasing income-producing properties and businesses.

As you work your way around the inside track of the board, you land on different squares. One square may be "paycheck" (where you receive your monthly salary, depending on your profession). Another square may be "opportunity" where you are presented with an investment opportunity such as a business, property, shares, or mutual funds. Another square may be "doodads." These are unexpected, often unnecessary expenses that require you to spend your money: for example, "Buy Big Screen TV, Pay $4000."

Once you have accumulated enough assets to generate a passive income that exceeds your living expenses, you're able to leave the "Rat Race" and play on the "Fast Track," located on the outer circle of the board game. Here, your goal is to realize the dream that you selected at the start. A few examples of the dream are "Golf around the world," "Be a jetsetter," "Have dinner with the President."

> The game of Cashflow® teaches us the importance of purchasing income-producing assets to get out of the "Rat Race."

How the Game Applies to Real Life

The focus of this book is on becoming wealthy so you can get out of the rat race. I will describe ways to understand, control, measure, and build wealth so that you can join others who are building their wealth. I will explain how to determine whether certain assets truly help you get out of the rat race, as well as how to structure deals to minimize the risk and maximize the upside, as well as cash flow.

I'm sure you've heard about many schemes. Different gurus say, "Start a home-based business," or "Buy real estate," or "Stay in mutual funds, stocks, and bonds." The question is, "Which is the real path to follow?"

My objective in this book is to focus on how to build wealth without using any specific investment vehicle. I will cut through all the products and assets and simply focus on the keys to building wealth. By the time you reach the end of the book, you will understand that building wealth can be simplified into very basic pieces, regardless of the vehicle used to generate wealth.

There are a lot of ideas out there about becoming wealthy. They are nothing more than someone's opinion of a vehicle that can make you wealthy. As long as you understand the core of building wealth, you will be able to filter out all the fluff and choose your own vehicle(s) to help you achieve your financial goals.

My Personal Goal

My goal in writing this book is to teach you what the wealthy do to become wealthy. It picks up where *Rich Dad Poor Dad* left off, walking you through the details of using "good debt" to become wealthy. As you will discover, there is more to "good debt" than most people realize. You will see wealth-building in a new and different way. For many, it will connect to what you may have read in the past.

I will also provide you with spreadsheets you will need to quantify some of the concepts I will be describing. This is a hands-on, "let's get our hands dirty" book. We are about to jump into the nitty-gritty of building wealth.

All I ask is that you read the book completely — from cover to cover — to get the most out of it. In fact, you may want to read it several times to absorb all of the information the book holds. Without question, it contains what every wealth-builder needs to know to become wealthy.

Are You My Target Audience?

The information I will be sharing may make you uncomfortable. Everyone has been conditioned to think a certain way. The information in this book will truly make you wealthy, not a comfortable member of the middle class. It is meant to make you one of the members of the Very Rich.

Why do I give you this warning? Because of some people's beliefs or mindsets, they just cannot deal with this information. For example, because this book will challenge your beliefs about debt, you may feel uncomfortable. If my advice is right for you, great; if it doesn't sit comfortably with you, that's OK too. I just want to share some really powerful information that has made many individuals wealthy.

What about the gurus on TV? They're actually talking to us about how to become a member of the middle class. Their message to the masses is very different from my message to you. In fact, when you compare their message to Kiyosaki's message, you'll find that it's very different. In fact, on a number of things, it's exactly the opposite!

That's because they're teaching you to be in the middle class. I'm not. Their message is saving money and becoming debt free; mine is not, as you will find out.

> The question you have to ask yourself is this: Do I want to be a member of the middle class or do I want to be rich? This is not a trick question. It is a very legitimate question. Your answer dictates which strategies you follow, so take some time to consider the question carefully after reading the book.

WHEN YOU ARE READY,
LET'S DIVE INTO *THE WEALTHY CODE.*

CHAPTER SUMMARY

- Have enough passive income to pay for your expenses.
- You need to understand how to control, measure, and build wealth.
- Aim to become wealthy before worrying about being rich.
- Read Robert Kiyosaki's book, *Rich Dad Poor Dad*.
- Focus on how to build wealth without using any specific investment vehicle.

CHAPTER TWO

It Started One Sunny California Day

YEARS AGO ONE OF MY MENTORS GAVE ME A GIFT THAT CHANGED MY life. I had been investing in real estate — foreclosures, rehabbing, flipping properties, plus what everyone else was doing out there and being taught in seminars around the country. As I walked into my mentor's office that day, I admit I went in with an attitude. I thought I was a *true* real-estate investor and, because my mentor sat behind a desk all day, he was not. But the next 90 minutes would change my life — and my "attitude."

> *"George, have a seat. I want to share some information with you — information you need to hear. I'm going to do you a big favor, and you'll thank me one day in the future once you 'get it.' The information I share with you will allow you to jump ahead of most so-called "real estate investors" and become financially free much faster. I'm about to share with you what you need to know to become wealthy."*
>
> *I sat down, and he started sharing information that really, really altered my life.*

The Big Picture of the Wealthy

My mentor grabbed a pen and paper and started drawing a grid. It looked like this:

APPRECIATION	CASH FLOW	CASH INFLUX
• Forced Appreciation • Timing Market • Normal Market • SFR in Appreciating Market • NEGATIVE Cash Flow	• Income Properties • Paper • Businesses	• Flipping • Foreclosure • Rehab • Wholesale
GOAL: *Build equity to turn into cash flow*	GOAL: *Passive income > expenses*	GOAL: *Fund appreciation and cash flow deals*
RICH	**WEALTHY**	**JOB**

FIGURE 1: The Big Picture of the Wealthy (I)

"This is what I refer to as the big picture of the wealthy," he explained. "Every time you do a deal, figure out which column it belongs in. The Appreciation column is for building your equity that eventually gets moved into the Cash Flow column. The Appreciation column is where most of your net worth comes from. The Cash Flow column is where your passive income comes from. The Cash Influx column might be transactions with one-time income. For example, buying a property that needs work, fixing it, and selling it for a one-time profit is Cash Influx. You get paid once."

Although this strategy could work for anything, the examples I'll provide will be from real estate because that's what I was doing at the time. Later in this book, I'll introduce you to other ways to apply this information to other vehicles and in greater detail.

APPRECIATION	CASH FLOW	CASH INFLUX
• Forced Appreciation • Timing Market • Normal Market • SFR in Appreciating Market • **NEGATIVE Cash Flow**	• Income Properties • Paper • Businesses	• Flipping • Foreclosure • Rehab • Wholesale
GOAL: *Build equity to turn into cash flow*	GOAL: *Passive income > expenses*	GOAL: *Fund appreciation and cash flow deals*
RICH	**WEALTHY**	**JOB**

FIGURE 2: **The Big Picture of the Wealthy (II)**

As he continued, my mentor pointed out that the biggest problem in the Appreciation column is that there can be negative cash flow and that it's even to be expected. If you do deals solely here, you might become rich (as the table shows) — *if* you can handle the negative cash flow. Most people can't. I know people with a high net worth (because of all the equity they had built from properties they had in the Appreciation column) who lost it all through a bad economy or too much negative cash flow.

My mentor added that the goal is to own $10 million worth of properties under the Appreciation column. However, you have to build that while building the Cash Flow column.

In California, where over the past 25 years real estate has appreciated an average of 8% (much higher than the nation's 6% average), $10 million worth of properties gives you $800,000 equity gain per year for which you didn't have to work. However, equity in and of itself doesn't do anything for you but increase your net worth. You can't eat it. You can't buy anything with it. You can, however, sell that equity or borrow against it. With the money generated from equity, you can buy more properties or other forms of income-producing investment vehicles.

What you *should* concentrate on is the Cash Flow column. This column contains income properties, paper, and low-tech businesses. Income properties, such as larger apartment buildings, are a great way to generate cash flow. Paper, as used here, is generating cash flow from paper products — for example, being a private lender. (I'll describe this later in more detail.) By low-tech business, my mentor was referring to businesses with no professional employees — e.g., no doctors, lawyers, or highly skilled workers. He suggested concentrating on low-skilled employees. In short, a low-tech business is everything that is not high tech!

> ## Remember:
> Wealthy = enough passive income
> to cover all living expenses and losses
> incurred by negative cash flow from assets
> in the Appreciation column.

"Too many real estate investors are stuck in the right-hand column," my mentor observed.

I could relate to that; I was stuck there myself at the time. I was using the influx of cash to pay my expenses. I had become dependent on it. I had to get the next deal to live on. Ninety-five percent of all investors are stuck in that same rut. So they go to seminars where the glitz and hoopla encourages them to buy more training sessions claiming to help them with the right-hand column.

Think about this: When you go to a seminar, on which column do most of them focus? The seminar leader usually teaches the techniques used for the right-hand column. I was already using these techniques and making OK money, but I was not living the lifestyle I wanted, with time for my family and leisure. Those seminar-givers simply had me trading one job for another! They used the glamour and the excitement of their presentation to blind me to what they were really selling: the sexy part of what turns out to still be a job.

Look at the right-hand column. Wholesale, foreclosures, rehabbing, short sales — all these are courses sold in seminars. To what do they translate? A job! If you aren't convinced, try not doing those for a month! No income will be generated! That's what I call a job.

I am *not* suggesting that you stay out of the right-hand column. I'm simply suggesting that you can't call this investing. It's speculating.

Further, I'm cautioning you not to get stuck in that column. Many people who started rehabbing properties (buying properties requiring a lot of work and fixing them) have never been able to get out of that *job* because they need the money to pay for their expenses.

"Focus on the middle column first," my mentor offered. When I asked what I was going to finance this with, since I was really kind of stuck in the right-hand column, he responded: "Therein you'll find the code to unlock the wealth you're looking for. You need to use OPM — Other People's Money — to buy the properties you need."

OPM stands for Other People's Money

There are three things to substitute for the right-hand column (Cash Influx).

1. Keep your day job and pay for columns one and two.
2. Learn to use OPM to invest in columns one or two.
3. Systemize the "job" in column three into a low-tech "business" that can fit under column two.

Low-tech businesses can be systemized so they work for you after they're up and running. Because I had been doing real estate deals for two years, I didn't have a job to keep, so I became an expert at raising other people's money. A little later in this book I'll share with you what you need to know about raising OPM.

In a nutshell, here's what I had learned so far:

- Most seminars sell you a job.
- Rather than buying their job, focus on the Cash Flow and Appreciation columns.
- Use the Cash Flow column to start generating passive income.
- Harvest equity in the Appreciation column to later buy income-producing assets in the Cash Flow column, to grow your cash flow, hence your wealth.

This process is the key to The Wealthy Code.

I know you're wondering just how you're going to be able to do all of the above. That's what this book is all about. I'll walk you, step by step, to the wealth you want to have. Most of this book will concentrate on the middle column — Cash Flow for building wealth.

Let's break wealth into its different components (see the figure below). Wealth is based on the cash flow that comes from arbitrage. Arbitrage is the difference (the spread) between the rate at which you borrow money and the rate at which you gain from investing that money.

For example, when you borrow money at 6% and invest it at 9%, you're making a 3% spread. That's called arbitrage. The arbitrage comes from leverage. Think of it as borrowed money.

I'll give you more detail later. Right now, just know that these are the components of wealth.

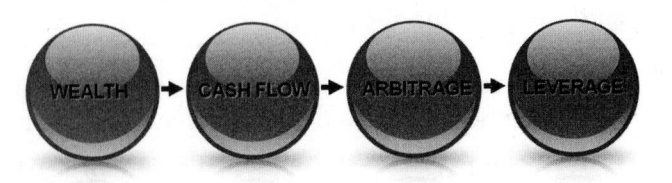

FIGURE 3: Breaking Wealth Into Basic Components

To reiterate, wealth is about generating more passive income than expenses. That's your cash flow. Cash flow is generated through spreads (or arbitrage). Arbitrage is a leveraged strategy. Leverage is using borrowed money to buy the assets that will generate your cash flow.

"And so" continued my mentor, "let's talk about leverage in more detail. But first, let's go to Chili's for lunch."

CHAPTER SUMMARY

Understand the "Big Picture of The Wealthy."
- Which column are you playing in today?
- Focus on the Cash Flow and Appreciation columns.
- Don't get stuck in the Cash Influx column.
- Replace the "job" in the Cash Influx column with one or more of three things:
  1. Keep your daytime job.
  2. Systemize one of the strategies under the Cash Influx column and turn it into a business that does not depend on you being there every day.
  3. Learn to raise OPM (Other People's Money).
- Understand that wealth comes from cash flow. Cash flow comes from arbitrage (or spreads). Arbitrage comes from leverage.

PART TWO

The Cash Flow Column

CHAPTER THREE

Dissecting Leverage

"So let me get this straight," I said as I sipped my Diet Coke at the restaurant. "To become wealthy, you need to have passive cash flow coming in. This is what Kiyosaki teaches in his book. But to generate that passive cash flow, you need to create a spread or arbitrage. To do that, you had better understand leverage. Isn't that what you just said?"

"That's right."

"So by understanding leverage, you will ultimately understand how to become wealthy. Am I saying that correctly?" I asked.

"Exactly. So, let's order our lunch and then talk about leverage."

THE FASTEST WAY TO GAIN WEALTH IS THROUGH LEVERAGE, THE RIGHT kind of leverage. And the fastest way to lose wealth is also with leverage, but the wrong kind of leverage. The problem today is that many people are using the wrong kind of leverage to build wealth, and they are setting themselves up to lose big money.

Experts tell us, "Leverage can make you rich!" That's partially true. However, what some of those experts are not telling us is how to find and use the right kind of leverage. The wrong kind of leverage can be devastating!

You've probably read this quote from the Greek mathematician, Archimedes: "Give me a lever and a place to stand, and I will move the earth." When we hear the word "leverage," what probably first comes to mind is the "lever" of which Archimedes spoke — *physical* leverage, an efficient way to move objects.

But *financial* leverage is what we use to control an entire asset with a small amount of money. It's really the use of borrowed money to purchase or control an asset.

> ## Financial leverage is what we use to control an entire asset using a small amount of money.

For example, in real estate, when you use a mortgage to buy a property, you are using leverage. Another way to think about it is that leverage allows individuals to purchase real estate with little, if any, of their own money. So it's the use of borrowed money to buy assets.

If we were to buy property using only our own cash, without obtaining a mortgage, we would not be using leverage. So unleveraged, in real estate, is buying a property using cash and without borrowing money. Having a mortgage is leveraged; paying all cash is unleveraged.

Leverage plays an important role in the cash flow (among other things) of the property. Leverage also plays an important role in the return on your investment.

Leverage = use of financing
Unleveraged = all cash
(no borrowed money)

An unnamed Guru's website states: "Leverage is the very common and safe practice of employing borrowed monies to increase your purchasing power, and thereby to multiply significantly the profitability of that investment."

Notice the use of the word "safe." That is just not true! Leverage can be great, but the minute you start working with leverage, it automatically increases your risk. The wrong kind of leverage can hurt you; the right kind can make you wealthy. The question to ask — and answer — is: "How do I work with leverage while understanding and controlling risk?" Hold that question; I'll cover it later.

Why Use Financial Leverage?

• Diversification benefits
• Ability to invest in multiple properties
• Mortgage interest tax benefits
• Magnify returns with the right leverage
• Become wealthier much faster

"Gentlemen, here are your burgers. Do you need a refill on your Diet Cokes as well?" inquired the waitress as she placed our food on the table.

"Sure. That would be great. Thanks," I replied as I began to attack my burger.

"Would you borrow money that would cost you $100 per month in interest to buy something that would pay you only $80 per month?" asked my mentor. I shook my head, not wanting to speak with my mouth full of burger.

"Now, would you borrow money that would cost you $100 per month in interest to buy something that would pay you $140 per month?" he asked again. I nodded in agreement this time.

"That's the difference between negative leverage and positive leverage. But you also have neutral leverage. ..."

"Wait!" I guess my mind had finally processed what it was I hadn't agreed with. "Nobody I know would borrow money at $100 per month in interest to make only $80 per month!"

He laughed, sat back, and set down his burger.

"Everyone is doing it, George. Few people understand it. Look around you. Most of these people here who own homes are doing it."

Types of Financial Leverage

I've referred to the "right" and the "wrong" kind of leverage. Let's consider that more closely.

Whenever I'm working with leverage, I make a comparison between an asset that's purchased with no leverage, meaning with all cash (unleveraged return), against that bought and financed (leveraged return). Let's call the all-cash return "Return X%" and the financed return "Return Y%." (See figure below.)

Compare Unleveraged Returns to Leveraged Returns

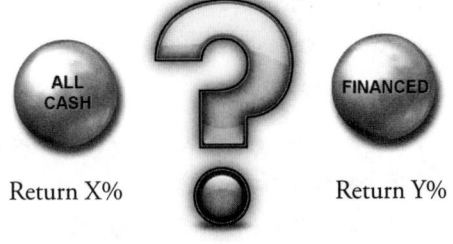

Return X%   Return Y%

FIGURE 4: Identifying Leverage by Comparing Returns

We need to compare X and Y in the image above. There are three possible results:

- X is smaller than Y   • X is the same as Y   • X is larger than Y

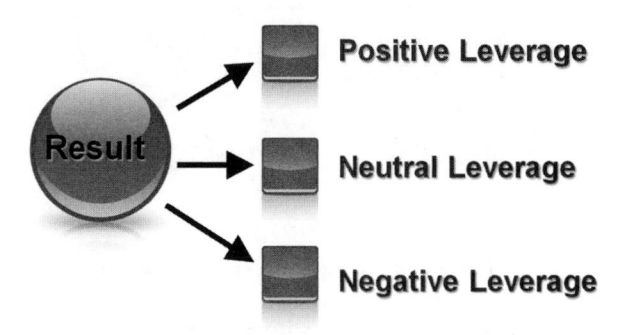

FIGURE 5: Leverage Possible Results

There are three possible leverage scenarios:

- Positive leverage
- Neutral leverage
- Negative leverage

Allow me to expand on this:

- **Positive leverage.** Leverage is positive if the investment return increases with debt financing. Basically, Y is greater than X. By borrowing money, our return is greater than if we do not borrow the money.

- **Neutral leverage.** Leverage is neutral if the investment return does not change with debt financing. Basically, Y is the same as X. By borrowing money, our return is the same as if we don't borrow money.

- **Negative Leverage.** Leverage is negative if the investment return decreases with debt financing. Basically, Y is less than X. By borrowing money, our return is lower than if we do not borrow any money.

Confused yet? All of this is just defining how hard your money is working for you. Let's look at an example.

Example One

Let's assume you decide to buy a property. You ask someone to calculate the leverage for you with a leverage calculator. You give this person all the details of the property and wait for him to give you the results. You then receive the two files shown in Figure 6.

File 1 is for a leveraged purchase (mortgage), and File 2 is for an unleveraged purchase (all cash). You realize that the return on the pur-

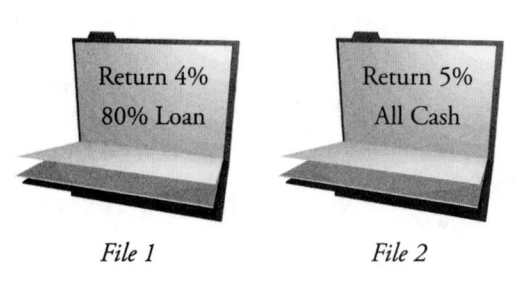

File 1   File 2

FIGURE 6: Example of Negative Leverage

chase with leverage is 4%. File 1 shows a return of 4% while obtaining an 80% loan (leverage). You also realize that the return on an all-cash (File 2) purchase is 5%. That means you are not using borrowed money to buy it. No mortgage whatsoever. This is an unleveraged purchase. Without knowing any more than what you see here, which return is better? The leveraged transaction or the unleveraged transaction?

Notice that in this example your return with the leveraged transaction (File 1) dropped compared to the unleveraged transaction (File 2), which is a classic example of negative leverage. That does *not* mean that you have negative cash flow; it simply means that the borrowed money is not working very hard for you. It also means that the financing is costing you more than the property is giving you. I'll deal with this in the next two chapters.

Example Two

You decide to change the structure of the financing. Again, you ask someone to calculate the leverage for you with a leverage calculator. As before, you receive two files (Figure 7).

The leveraged File 1 shows a 6% return on an 80% loan; the File 2 all-cash (unleveraged) return is 5%. Notice that the return on the leveraged File 1 is higher than the return on the unleveraged File 2. This is called positive leverage. This means that your dollars are working hard; the financing is working for you.

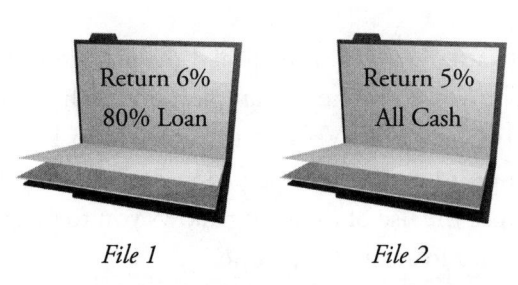

File 1   *File 2*

FIGURE 7: Example of Positive Leverage

So when the return is higher on the leveraged transaction (with borrowed money) than on the unleveraged transaction, the leverage is said to be positive. If the return is lower, it is said to be negative leverage.

Example Three

You decide to change the structure of your financing package once again. Then you ask someone to use a leverage calculator to figure out the leverage for you. And again, you receive two files (Figure 8).

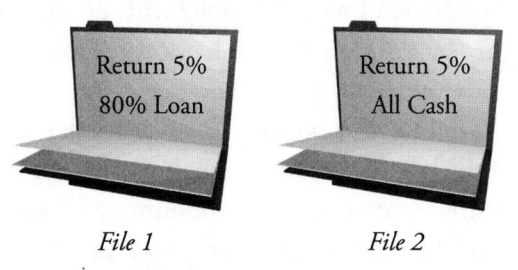

File 1   *File 2*

FIGURE 8: Example of Neutral Leverage

As before, in File 2 the all-cash return is 5%. This time, however, File 1 shows a 5% return on an 80% loan. Notice that the return of the leveraged file is the same as that of the unleveraged file. This is an example of neutral leverage.

To reiterate:

POSITIVE LEVERAGE: Leverage is positive if the investment return increases with borrowed money. All cash = 5% return, and the 80% loan of Example Two shows a 6% return.

NEUTRAL LEVERAGE: Leverage is neutral if the investment return does not change with borrowed money. Example Three, where all-cash gives a 5% return and the 80% LTV (loan-to-value) ratio loan gives a 5% return, is an example of neutral leverage. However, this is not necessarily a bad thing, because the use of financing allows you to put your money into many properties instead of only one.

NEGATIVE LEVERAGE: Leverage is negative if the investment return decreases with borrowed money. In Example One, the all-cash return is 5%, but the 80% LTV loan gives only a 4% return. Essentially, the financing is costing more than the return, and you are not using your money as efficiently as you could be.

Now, here's a question to think about. Is positive leverage the only way to get positive cash flow? The answer is no. You can get positive cash flow even with a deal based on negative leverage. But your money is not being used as effectively as it could be. Unbeknownst to many investors, one of the reasons lenders ask for a large down payment is that they know they are lending you money with negative leverage. So the down payment is a cushion for the lenders to protect themselves! I'll explain that in the next two chapters.

Of course, you would prefer positive leverage so that your cash flow can be greater and the borrowed money will be working for you instead of against you. With negative leverage the money is working against you, but you still could have positive cash flow. The difference might be that with positive leverage your income may go up to $1,600 per month, and with negative leverage your income may be only $900 per month.

Here is another question to think about. Is negative leverage always bad? Again, the answer is no. If you are buying for a quick flip (buying and selling a house quickly), you may not even care. If you're looking at a long-term finance, you want to have positive leverage, but for the short-term it won't make a big difference.

The key is to understand that positive leverage applies to assets you're buying for the Cash Flow column, and that long-term holds for the Appreciation column.

"That was good!" exclaimed my mentor.

"You're right! This is great information," I said excitedly.

"I was referring to the burger and fries," my mentor laughed as he sat back into his seat. "Can you hand me a napkin please?" he asked as he looked up at the television.

CHAPTER SUMMARY

- Financial leverage = Use of borrowed money.
- No leverage = Use of all cash; no borrowed money.
- Positive leverage = Leverage is positive if the investment return increases with the use of borrowed money compared to the return without the borrowed money.
- Neutral leverage = Leverage is neutral if the investment return does not change with the use of borrowed money compared to the return without the borrowed money.
- Negative leverage = Leverage is negative if the investment return decreases with the use of borrowed money compared to the return without the borrowed money.
- As wealth builders, we want to use positive leverage in our investments.
- The key is to understand that positive leverage applies to assets you are buying for the Cash Flow column and that long-term holds for the Appreciation column.

CHAPTER FOUR

Calculating Leverage

"Look at that!" exclaimed my mentor as he looked up to watch the football game. Chili's bar had several TV sets, and everyone in the bar seemed glued to the game. I couldn't have cared less about the game. The information I was "downloading" was life-changing.

"That was great," I offered as I also looked up at the television, pretending to show excitement. I didn't even know who was playing.

"Okay, George. I'm going to share with you some pretty interesting information that the wealthy have used to become wealthy. But we have to cover some basics first. So let me show you how to calculate leverage," he said as he searched his pockets for a piece of paper and pen.

I knew I had to be patient to get to the good stuff.

"Miss, can we have a few sheets of paper and a pen?" I asked the waitress.

TO CALCULATE LEVERAGE, WE MUST START BY UNDERSTANDING AND calculating returns. Returns are important because they give us an indication of how well our investment is performing or will perform. As wealth builders, we are obviously looking for higher returns.

Calculating Returns

One can calculate many types of returns for an investment, but I'm going to use a simple cash-on-cash return. This is the annual cash flow coming in from an investment (such as property or any other asset). To calculate the return, take whatever the investment pays you at the end of the year (after paying the mortgage, expenses, and everything else) and divide it by the original investment from your pocket. This is the simple formula that will give us our return: Cash-on-cash return = annual cash flow/money invested.

Remember, the annual cash flow is what's left in our pocket at the end of the year after paying all expenses and loans. This is also called a pre-tax, cash-on-cash return because we have not paid taxes on it yet (i.e., capital gains).

Let's say that a property has a cash flow per year of $5,000 after the mortgage and all expenses have been paid. This is your annual cash flow. Let's also say that the money you had invested was $100,000 — including the down payment and everything that went into buying the property. So your cash-on-cash return is calculated by dividing the $5,000 cash flow by the out-of-pocket investment of $100,000 (cash-on-cash return = $5,000/$100,000) — a 5% return.

Obviously, the higher the cash-on-cash return, the better off you are as an investor.

Measuring Leverage

In the previous chapter, I began to explain the importance of comparing leveraged return to unleveraged return.

> ## Measuring Leverage
> Compare all-cash return (x%) with
> financed return (y%).

Soon, we'll start using the Simple Financial Leverage Calculator. I mention that because we're going to jump into some numbers here — doing the math! Don't be concerned; this free calculator can do all the calculations for you. So go through the examples, and don't worry about the exact calculations. Just understand the main concepts.

Using the calculator, we'll be reviewing positive leverage, neutral leverage, and negative leverage.

Let's use this small table to illustrate an example.

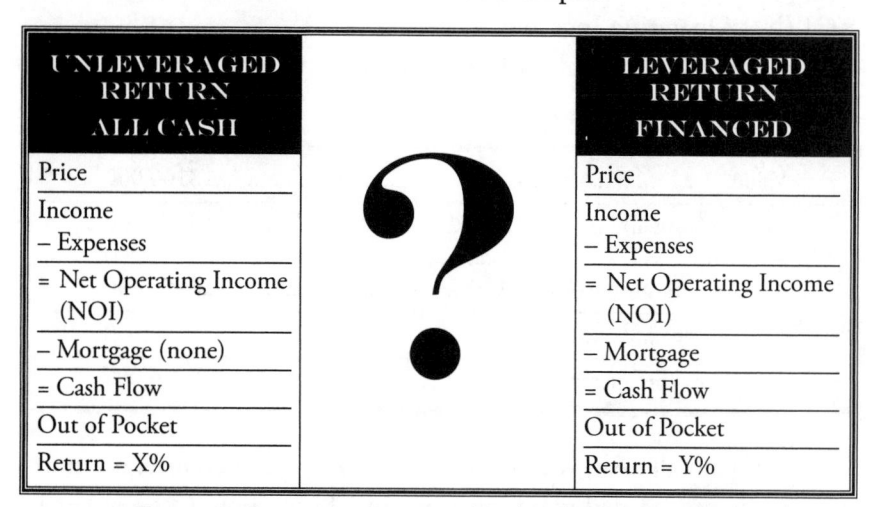

FIGURE 9: Comparing Leveraged and Unleveraged Return

Value of Asset	$100,000
Income (annual)	$ 10,000
Expenses	$ 4,000
Net Operating Income (NOI)	$ 6,000

So, assume you have an asset valued at $100,000 that's generating an income of $10,000 per year. The expenses are $4,000 per year. The difference, also known as the Net Operating Income (NOI), is $10,000 – $4,000, or $6,000 per year.

NOI = Income – Expenses

The mortgage payments are not included in the expenses. Expenses can be broken into six main categories, which I call by the mnemonic, TIM-MUR: taxes (property taxes), insurance, management, maintenance, utilities, and repair. Mortgage payments are actually deducted from the NOI (Net Operating Income).

Now, if you had paid all cash for this property, your table would look like this:

Value...	$100,000
Income (annual)	$ 10,000
– Expenses	$ 4,000
= Net Operating Income (NOI)...	$ 6,000
– Mortgage	$ 0
Cash Flow (before taxes)	$ 6,000

Since you paid all cash, you don't have a mortgage; therefore, no mortgage payments are deducted. So the annual cash flow (money left in your pocket at the end of the year) is $6,000.

The cash-on-cash return would be equal to the annual cash flow divided by the money invested, as described before. Since the return is $6,000, we'll divide it by $100,000 (we paid all cash for the property) to find that you have a 6% cash-on-cash return. This would be an illustration of the left side of fig. 9 (page 33).

To calculate the right side of fig. 9 (the leveraged side using financing), we'll measure the return *with* the debt (borrowed money). Assume a 20% down payment and a loan of $80,000 (80% loan) at 6% amortized over 30 years. Plug those numbers in the calculator. The annual mortgage payments are $5,760.

Value...$100,000	
Income ....$ 10,000	
– Expenses (TIMMUR)....................................$ 4,000	
= NOI ....$ 6,000	
– Mortgage ....$ 5,760	
Cash Flow...$ 240	

What will be the cash-on-cash return in this situation? Remember our formula: the return is equal to the annual cash flow divided by the money invested. In this case, $240 divided by $20,000 is equal to 1.2%.

Cash-on-cash = $240/$20,000 = 1.2%

So, at the end of one year you have all-cash, cash-on-cash return of 6% compared to the financed-buy, cash-on-cash return of 1.2%. With the loan, your return dropped. This is an example of negative leverage. It's also the way many people are buying properties and other assets — with negative leverage — and they have no idea that's what they're doing.

If, however, with the 80% loan in place, the cash flow were $1,400 per year, you would get a return of 7%.

Cash-on-cash = $1400/$20,000 = 7.0%

So, a leveraged purchase would give you a return of 7%, whereas an all cash purchase would be equal to a return of 6%.

Therefore, the X percentage in fig. 9 would be 6% on an unleveraged property, and the Y percentage would be 7% on a leveraged property, showing an example of a positive leverage. (This is just for the purpose of an example and is not based on real numbers.)

The Simple Financial Leverage Calculator

The Simple Financial Leverage Calculator is a calculator that does all the calculations for you. You can download it from our website at no cost. Please refer to the Resources section in the back of this book (page 159) for download information.

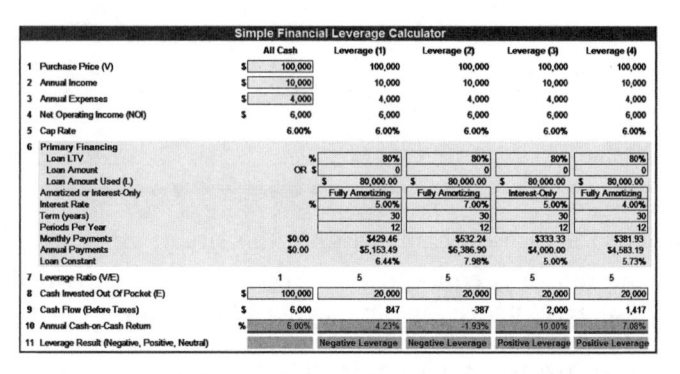

		All Cash	Leverage (1)	Leverage (2)	Leverage (3)	Leverage (4)
1	Purchase Price (V)	$ 100,000	100,000	100,000	100,000	100,000
2	Annual Income	$ 10,000	10,000	10,000	10,000	10,000
3	Annual Expenses	$ 4,000	4,000	4,000	4,000	4,000
4	Net Operating Income (NOI)	$ 6,000	6,000	6,000	6,000	6,000
5	Cap Rate	6.00%	6.00%	6.00%	6.00%	6.00%
6	**Primary Financing**					
	Loan LTV	%	80%	80%	80%	80%
	Loan Amount	OR $	0	0	0	0
	Loan Amount Used (L)	$	80,000.00	$ 80,000.00	$ 80,000.00	$ 80,000.00
	Amortized or Interest-Only		Fully Amortizing	Fully Amortizing	Interest-Only	Fully Amortizing
	Interest Rate	%	5.00%	7.00%	5.00%	4.00%
	Term (years)		30	30	30	30
	Periods Per Year		12	12	12	12
	Monthly Payments	$0.00	$429.46	$532.24	$333.33	$381.93
	Annual Payments	$0.00	$5,153.49	$6,386.90	$4,000.00	$4,583.19
	Loan Constant		6.44%	7.98%	5.00%	5.73%
7	Leverage Ratio (V/E)	1	5	5	5	5
8	Cash Invested Out Of Pocket (E)	$ 100,000	20,000	20,000	20,000	20,000
9	Cash Flow (Before Taxes)	$ 6,000	847	-387	2,000	1,417
10	Annual Cash-on-Cash Return	% 6.00%	4.23%	-1.93%	10.00%	7.08%
11	Leverage Result (Negative, Positive, Neutral)		Negative Leverage	Negative Leverage	Positive Leverage	Positive Leverage

FIGURE 10: The Simple Financial Leverage Calculator

The Simple Financial Leverage Calculator is for comparing all-cash purchases to various scenarios of leveraged purchases.

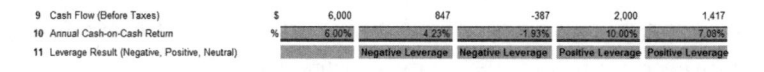

9	Cash Flow (Before Taxes)	$	6,000	847	-387	2,000	1,417
10	Annual Cash-on-Cash Return	%	6.00%	4.23%	-1.93%	10.00%	7.08%
11	Leverage Result (Negative, Positive, Neutral)			Negative Leverage	Negative Leverage	Positive Leverage	Positive Leverage

FIGURE 11: Partial Calculator Output

Figure 11 shows a part of the calculator output. It gives you the cash-on-cash return and whether the leverage you entered is positive, negative, or neutral.

You'll notice that leverage is all about picking the right loan. Sometimes it doesn't seem so clear which loan is the best one for any single deal. The Simple Financial Leverage Calculator will make that much clearer. I'll explain a little further on how you go about picking the right numbers to make the best deal.

As for using the calculator, use the yellow (shown here in lighter gray) areas to enter data. All the other non-yellow sections will automatically be calculated for you, depending on the data you enter in the yellow areas.

For more information on the Calculator and its uses, refer to the Resources section.

"Are you crazy mathematicians or something?" laughed the waitress as she passed our table. About a dozen pages filled with scribbles, diagrams, and computations were scattered all over our table.

"No, we're designing a money machine!" I replied with a smile. "A money machine that spits out money monthly."

CHAPTER SUMMARY

- To measure leverage, you must measure returns.
- Cash-on-cash return = annual cash flow/money invested.
- Leverage has an effect on the return of an investment.
- The return of an unleveraged investment must be compared to the return of various leveraged scenarios to determine which one to use.
- The Simple Financial Leverage Calculator can be downloaded for free. Refer to the Resources section for more information.

CHAPTER FIVE

Maximizing Your Cash Flow

"Are you absorbing all this?" asked my mentor, while munching on his fries.

"Bring it on man! I'm with you. I can handle this. Keep it coming!" I chuckled as I began to write on yet another blank sheet. I had been writing furiously to get all this information down.

This reminded me of my previous experience designing software applications. I had spent years with software companies developing solutions by starting with a new, clean notebook that ended up with hundreds of computations and diagrams for each project.

At one of the companies I consulted with, Intuit, makers of Quicken, America's no. 1 personal finance software, I had helped develop software for people to manage their finances and plan their retirement. Everything I was writing down with my mentor reminded me of those days.

Leverage affects four areas, as shown on the image below.

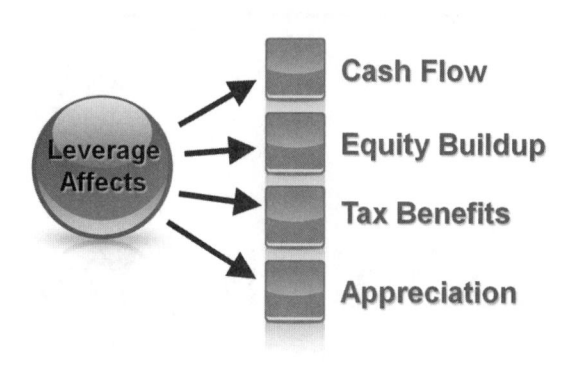

FIGURE 12: Leverage Affects All Profit Centers

Cash Flow: Cash flow refers to the movement of cash into or out of a business, a project, or a financial product. It's usually measured during a specified, finite period of time; in this case, I'm talking about how much money is left after paying all expenses and borrowed money. I'm also focusing on how leverage increases or decreases the cash flow as a rate of return. More on cash flow later in this chapter.

Equity Buildup: Equity buildup is the increase in the investor's equity as the portion of mortgage payments devoted to principal accrue over time. Equity buildup occurs when the mortgage payment is made. In the process, it pays down the mortgage, which in turn generates more equity for us. In this instance, I'm talking about how leverage affects equity buildup as a return on the money invested. I will not be covering equity buildup in this book.

Tax: In this case, I'm talking about how leverage affects tax savings due to ownership of property. Nor do I cover taxes in this book.

Appreciation: Appreciation generally occurs over time, though an investor may "force the equity" in a property by making enhancements to it (or the surrounding environment) to increase its value or buy it under market value to create instant equity. Here, I'm referring to how leverage affects the rates of return for appreciation. I'll provide more detail on this in Chapter 6.

In the previous chapter I covered the differences between an all-cash asset purchase and the reasons for getting a loan to spread out your money and make it work harder for you. I showed you a table comparing an unleveraged purchase and a leveraged purchase and how these two can affect positive and negative cash flow.

In this chapter I'm going to explain how to squeeze out more cash flow by using leverage. I'll also show you, using the Simple Financial Leverage Calculator, how the four profit centers affect each other to give you a higher or lower return, based on the leverage. To have a positive return in each area, you need to know how to select the best leverage for each deal or purchase you make. And that's exactly what I'm sharing with you — how to select the best leverage so that you can reach the level of "wealthy" faster.

Also in this chapter, I'll be covering the ups and downs of cash flow and how to maintain, measure, and increase it.

In the next chapter I'll explain how leverage affects returns on appreciation and how you could go about controlling it. Both of these areas will have strong influences on the other two profit centers mentioned above: your build-up of equity and your tax benefits.

When you begin to recognize and understand details that escape the beginner's eye, you're on your way to being a savvy investor, one who makes decisions based on knowledge instead of gut reactions or uneducated guesses. To help you get to that point, I'll be focusing on what's going on behind the scenes.

The Special ATM Example

You walk into your local retail store and find two ATMs on sale. They look identical, but the one on the left has a price tag of $120,000, and the one on the right has a price tag of $70,000. (Remember the price of each machine!) These are special ATM machines; when you stand in front of each of them on the first day of every month, they spit out cash. The one on the left releases $1,000 per month; the one on the right releases $500 per month.

So, which ATM machine is the better deal? Which should you buy?

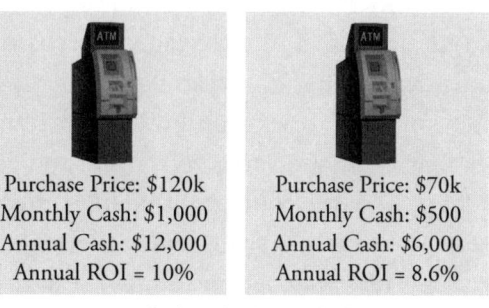

Purchase Price: $120k	Purchase Price: $70k
Monthly Cash: $1,000	Monthly Cash: $500
Annual Cash: $12,000	Annual Cash: $6,000
Annual ROI = 10%	Annual ROI = 8.6%

Which is the better deal?

FIGURE 13: Two "Special" ATM Machines On Sale

Let me give you a hint — the annual cash flow of the one on the left is $12,000 — that is the monthly cash flow multiplied by 12. The one on the right has an annual cash flow of $6,000. What we learned about how to find the return is to divide the annual cash flow by the purchase (all-cash outright) price for the return. That makes the return of the ATM on the left, 10% ($12k/$120k); the return on the one on the right is 8.6% ($6k/$70k).

Assuming you had the money to buy one of them, which is the better deal?

ATM left: Annual return = $12,000/$120,000 = 10%

ATM right: Annual return = $6,000/$70,000 = 8.6%

Obviously, the one on the left with the 10% return is a better deal than the 8.6% ATM machine, assuming you had the cash for it. However, let's now assume you do not have the cash.

You know the ATM on the left generates 10% return if you purchase it all-cash.

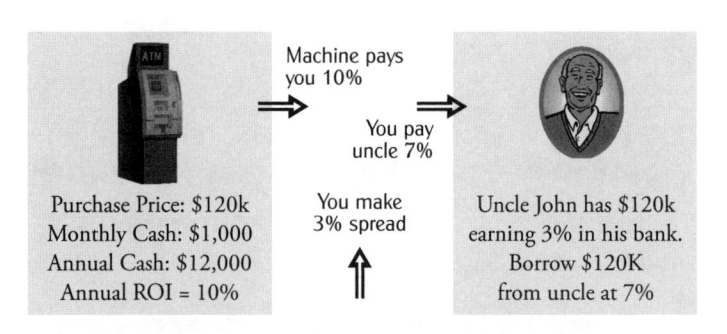

FIGURE 14: How Would You *Buy* This ATM Machine?

Let's assume you have an Uncle John who loves you as his favorite nephew or niece. And this wonderful Uncle John has $120,000 in the bank getting a mere 3% interest rate. You ask him to lend you that $120,000 at 7%. You offer to secure his loan to you by the ATM machine.

Uncle John writes you a check in a minute, beaming about what a bright child you have always been. You run to your bank to deposit this check, and then you run right down to your retail store and write a check for the ATM machine that will give you the better return.

The ATM machine pays you 10% and you pay Uncle John 7%. When, on the first of the month, the machine releases $1,000, you pay a predetermined amount to Uncle John ($700), giving you a 3% spread ($300).

This, in essence, is what you want each and every purchase to do for you. Borrow money at a lower rate, and get a spread (or arbitrage) that will provide you with passive income.

The technical term used in real estate for the percentage of income a property generates to the price paid for it is the "capitalization rate" (cap rate), or 10% in our example.

The term for the measure of cash outflow going to pay the loan is "loan constant." The loan constant is not the interest rate. (Sometimes the loan constant can equal the interest rate, but it is not the same thing.) It is the annual cash outflow as a percentage of the loan amount. More on this later.

In our example:

$$\text{Spread \$} = \text{Cash inflow} - \text{Cash outflow}$$
$$\text{Spread \%} = \text{Cap rate} - \text{Loan constant}$$

$$\text{Spread \$} = \$1,000 - \$700 = \$300$$

$$\text{Spread \%} = 10\% - 7\% = 3\%$$

The spread is that difference between the cap rate of the asset (ATM machine) and the loan constant you are paying for the leverage. In this case, what you get from the machine is 10%, and what you pay back to Uncle John is 7%, so you earn a spread of 3%.

For now, to simplify this, think of the cap rate as the percentage that an asset pays you and the loan constant as the percentage you pay for the borrowed money. So associate cap rate with assets and loan constants with borrowed money.

Apartment Building Example

Let's dip our toe into the real estate market. Consider a 20-unit apartment building in a great location with historically great management and occupancy. Let's assume this particular property has a 9% cap rate (what it would give you if you bought it all cash — just like the ATM machines). You don't have the cash, so you look for a lender.

Looking around, you find a lender that will lend you the money. The loan constant of this loan is 7%, so you end up making a 2% spread.

To reiterate, when you make any purchase, you need to measure the cap rate and the loan constant to get the best spread. That is the essence of an income property or business.

Think of cap rates and loan constants as two sides of the ledger (In versus Out) or as two widgets. The following must occur to create positive leverage:

> **To maximize cash flow, and ultimately wealth, you need to be able to measure the cap rate of an asset (property) and the loan constant of the leverage. This allows you to calculate your spread.**

- The interest rate and the loan constant on the leverage must be lower than the capitalization rate.
- The spread (arbitrage) generates the passive cash flow.

Understanding the Loan Constant

As explained above, the loan constant is not the interest rate; it is the annual cash outflow as a percentage of the loan amount. To calculate the loan constant, simply use The Simple Financial Leverage Calculator.

So, if you were to borrow $100,000 and your payments would be $7,200 per year (regardless of the interest rate), your loan constant is 7.2%.

> **Your loan constant is a measure of your annual cash outflow.**

The following loans both give you a 7.2% loan constant:

$100,000 at 7.2% interest only

$100,000 at 6% amortized over 30 years

Why? Because they both generate annual cash payments of $7,200 per year (numbers rounded for example).

So once again, loan constant is the annual cash going out of your pocket, regardless of how much principal or interest, divided by the loan amount.

Loan constant = Annual loan payment/Loan amount

The formula above is for annual loan constant. You can also calculate the monthly loan constant. However, for the purposes of this book, I will use "annual loan constant" and "loan constant" interchangeably. I will *not* use monthly loan constant.

Anytime you are dealing with assets in the Cash Flow column, you have to maximize the cash flow. You do so by comparing the property's capitalization rate and the loan constant. Most people use the interest rate on the loan as a primary gauge of leverage. This is one of the biggest problems many investors have — comparing interest rates instead of loan constants.

If you find a property with a cap rate of 5% and your leverage loan constant is 7%, you have a negative spread of 2%. This is an example of negative leverage.

If the cap rate is 7% and the loan constant is 7%, you have no spread. This is an example of neutral leverage.

Calculating this is pretty easy.

LOAN 1	LOAN 2	LOAN 3	LOAN 4
5.5%	6.8%	8.2%	7.8%
5-year fixed amortized	30-year fixed amortized	10-year fixed interest-only	15-year fixed amortized

Which loan has the lowest loan constant?
FIGURE 15: EXAMPLE OF LOAN CONSTANTS (I)

Which loan (above) is the best loan for a building with a 9% cap rate? Another way to ask the question is, "Which one has the lowest loan constant?" Hint: You'll need a calculator.

LOAN 1	LOAN 2	LOAN 3	LOAN 4
5.5%	6.8%	8.2%	7.8%
5-year fixed amortized	30-year fixed amortized	10-year fixed interest-only	15-year fixed amortized
22.92%	7.82%	8.2%	11.33%

Which loan has the lowest loan constant?
FIGURE 16: Example of Loan Constants (II)

Notice that loan no. 2 has the lowest loan constant, which makes it ideal for the 9% cap rate property I mentioned earlier. It maximizes the spread (9% – 7.82%). Notice also that loan no. 1 has the lowest interest rate at 5.5%, yet because it has the highest loan constant, it is the worst loan when it comes to maximizing cash flow.

Unfortunately, many investors pick the wrong loans based on interest rate alone, which ends up being devastating.

Never ask a mortgage broker for a single loan quote. He or she will quote the loan that pays him or her the best rate, and not you. In fig. 16, you see four loan quotes. Get as many quotes as you can from the lender and plug them into the free calculator we provide to figure out which one is best for you.

In conclusion, anytime you are dealing with borrowed money that is being used to buy an asset that generates cash flow, always calculate the loan constant.

Understanding the Capitalization Rate

We also need to learn how to calculate the cap rate of any property. Many people think that cap rates apply only to commercial properties. Not so. Anytime you're buying for cash flow (for a spread) you need to look at the cap rate of the asset you are buying and the loan constant of the leverage you are using.

Whenever you are looking at a property, there are a number of pieces of data you need to be thinking about.

Cap Rate Example 1

Consider the numbers in the example below.

Property Price =	**$550,000** ⟸
Income	$100,000
Expenses	− $ 45,000
NOI	$ 55,000 ⟸
Mortgage Payments	− $ 44,000
Cash Flow	$ 11,000

CapRate = NOI/Price = $55k/$550k = 10%

FIGURE 17: Cap Rate (Example 1)

All expenses (TIMMUR as described before, less mortgage payments) are included.

> ## The property price and the NOI (Net Operating Income) are very important in determining the cap rate.
> ## Cap rate = NOI/Price

In the example above, the price is $550,000, and the NOI is $55,000. The cap rate is calculated by dividing the Net Operating Income (NOI) by the price. Refer to the figure above for calculation of the cap rate.

Cap Rate Example 2

Consider the numbers in the example below.

Property Price =	**$100,000**
Income	$ 10,000
Expenses	– $ 4,000
NOI	$ **6,000**
Mortgage Payments	– $ 4,000
Cash Flow	$ 2,000

CapRate = NOI/Price = $6k/$100k = 6%

FIGURE 18: Cap Rate (Example 2)

The Simple Leverage Loan Calculator allows you to calculate all of the above. The NOI is the difference between the income and the expenses. In this example, it's $6000. The price of the property is $100,000; therefore, the cap rate is 6% (calculation shown above).

Why is it important to know the cap rate? Remember, I said that to obtain the best loan (leverage) for any asset purchase, you must compare the cap rate with the loan constant. I make students remember this phrase: "Assets are to cap rates as leverage is to loan constants."

Real Life Example

What you've learned so far is to calculate the loan constant and the cap rate. You should now understand that the greater the spread, the greater the cash flow.

> ## The greater the spread, the greater the cash flow, and the greater the return.

Let's look at an actual example a student brought to me for evaluation. The student owned a house and wanted to refinance it to pull money out for the down payment on a fourplex (4 units) that he would use for cash flow — his primary objective. He decided to refinance the house to get the 20% down payment needed to purchase the fourplex. In addition, he took out a conventional loan for 80% to be used in purchasing the structure.

This particular fourplex, in San Jose, Calif., had a capitalization rate of 2%. The money he obtained from refinancing his house (for the down payment) had a loan constant of 6%. The conventional 80% LTV loan had a loan constant of 6.5%.

So the student had borrowed 100% of the money at a loan constant much *higher* than the capitalization rate of the fourplex. It should be obvious that the asset will *not* generate positive cash flow.

But the real estate agent convinced him to buy it. Unfortunately, he listened because the agent was the "expert," and in the agent's view, fourplexes did not use cap rates.

Don't ask what happened!

Remember this: No matter what building you are buying, if your primary objective is to develop cash flow, you have to look at both cap rate and loan constant. Forget what the real estate agent might tell you about not using cap rates. This is how cash flow is generated!

What Positive Leverage Deals Look Like

Here's another example. A property has a 9% cap rate. You get institutional financing at 7.5% loan constant for the first 80% LTV. You get seller financing (you agree to pay the seller over time and not immediately — basically borrowing from the seller) at 7.0% loan constant for the second 10% LTV. On both loans, the loan constant is lower than the cap rate. This is positive leverage *maximizing* your cash flow return. This is what savvy investors do. This is positive leverage all around.

Summary

Compare the cap rate of the asset with the loan constant of the borrowed money (leverage). The loan constant *must* be lower than the cap rate, and then you can look for the best (highest) spread in order to maximize cash flow.

In this chapter we were looking only at how leverage affects cash flow. In the next chapter we'll be investigating how leverage affects appreciation.

"You mean there's more?" I asked, as we returned to his office.

"We haven't even started!" my mentor laughed. "Are you doing OK with all this?"

"Well, keep going. My arm might fall off from writer's cramp, but other than that, keep going."

CHAPTER SUMMARY

- Leverage affects four components:
  1. Cash Flow
  2. Equity buildup
  3. Tax
  4. Appreciation
- We focused on the effects of leverage on cash flow alone.
- You can use leverage to create a nice cash flow stream.
- To use positive leverage, make sure the cap rate of the asset is higher than the loan constant of the leverage.
- The higher the spread, the more passive cash flow you can put in your pocket.
- The result of this positive leverage allows for higher cash-on-cash return and passive income.
- The larger the spread, the higher the cash-on-cash return.

CHAPTER SIX

Maximizing Your Net Worth

"Well, let's get into some fun stuff now!" My mentor's enthusiasm was contagious. "This you will like a lot! I assume you know what compounding is, right? You've probably heard of Albert Einstein's quote about compounding being the eighth wonder of the world."

"Yup. What about it?"

"Well, start writing. This you do not want to miss."

IN THE PREVIOUS CHAPTER I EXPLAINED HOW LEVERAGE AFFECTS YOUR return from cash flow. In this chapter I will cover how leverage affects your return from appreciation and ultimately maximizes your net worth. Remember that leverage affects your returns from four profit centers in real estate: cash flow, equity buildup, tax, and appreciation.

Appreciation and Interest Rates

Your goal is to have the interest rate on the loan (leverage) be the same or lower than the projected appreciation rate on the property. This does not have to be true in every case, but it's preferable.

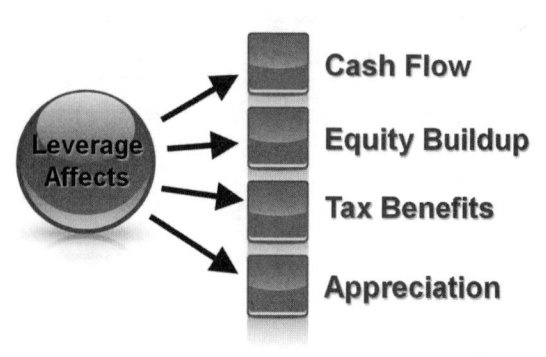

FIGURE 19: Leverage Affects All Profit Centers

For example, if the appreciation in an area has been historically 6%, the target interest rate you aim for is 6% or less. We're not talking about the loan constant here, rather, the interest rate.

> To maximize our return from appreciation, interest rate on the leverage should be less than or equal to the projected appreciation rate.

Here's something to keep in mind. The monthly mortgage payment is normally the same (fixed), but appreciation is compounding. This is powerful! When you borrow money at simple interest and invest in a compounding investment, you make a lot of money. This is a way to compare the mortgage versus appreciation. Mortgage is not really simple interest; instead, it's usually a fixed monthly payment.

The chart below illustrates the effect of the property value compounding over 30 years versus the cumulative interest paid over the same 30-year period. The Simple Leverage Loan Calculator will allow you to experiment with those numbers.

The chart shows the value of the property growing much faster over time than what we paid for it in interest. In other words, we're using leverage to maximize our net worth (building equity). This is the beauty of using leverage with fixed payments to invest into a compounding asset. The results are tremendous!

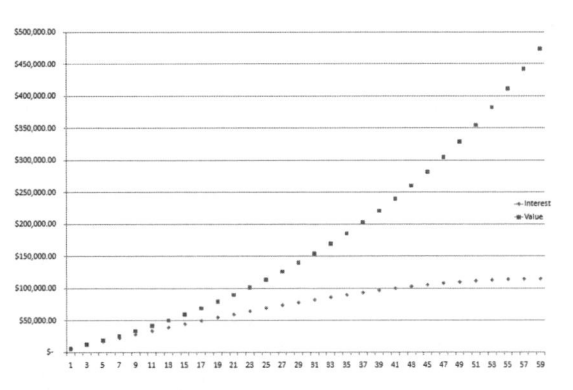

FIGURE 20: Chart of Property Value and Cumulative Interest Paid

For example, let's assume a property valued at $100,000 with a mortgage of $100,000 on the property (100% loan to value). I'll assume that for the purpose of illustrating the effects of leverage, but I recognize you cannot easily get 100% LTV loans for an investment property. The mortgage is amortized over 30 years at 7%. Assume the appreciation rate is 5%.

Property Value	$100,000.00
Amortized or Interest-Only..................................	Fully Amortized
Loan Amount	$100,000.00
Number of Payments Per Year............................	12
Years	30
Interest	7.00%
Monthly Payment (P&I)......................................	$ 661.44
Appreciation...	5.00%
Mortgage Payments..	$ 7,937.33
First Year Appreciation	$ 5,000.00

FIGURE 21: Example of Data Entered Into Calculator

DATA

Property Value	$100,000.00
Amortized or Interest-Only	Fully Amortized
Loan Amount	$100,000.00
No. of Payments Per Year	12
Years	30
Interest	7.00%
Monthly Payment (P&I)	$ 661.44
Appreciation	5.00%
Mortgage Payments	$ 7,937.33
First Year Appreciation	$ 5,000.00

"+L" means POSITIVE LEVERAGE

"-L" means NEGATIVE LEVERAGE

This does *not* consider Cashflow Leverage; it strictly looks at Appreciation Leverage. Also, in this calculator, we use the assumption that the loan is 100% LTV of the value to highlight the effect on the value. So "Cost of Money" (Cumulative Interest) is looking at INTEREST alone (even if loan is amortized) and assumes 100% loan. It does *not* matter if loan is 100% loan. It does *not* matter if loan is 100% LTV, but for sake of calculating the leverage result, we use that.

MORTGAGE PAYMENTS

YEAR	CUMULATIVE MONEY PAID	CUMULATIVE INTEREST PAID	LEVERAGE
1	$ 7,937.33	$ 6,347.46	-L
2	$ 15,874.66	$ 13,201.86	-L
3	$ 23,811.99	$ 19,977.98	-L
4	$ 31,749.32	$ 26,670.16	-L
5	$ 39,686.64	$ 33,272.32	-L
6	$ 47,623.97	$ 39,777.96	-L
7	$ 55,561.30	$ 46,180.11	-L
8	$ 63,498.63	$ 52,471.27	-L
9	$ 71,435.96	$ 58,643.44	-L
10	$ 79,373.29	$ 64,688.00	-L
11	$ 87,310.62	$ 70,595.74	+L
12	$ 95,247.95	$ 76,356.75	+L
13	$ 103,185.28	$ 81,960.44	+L
14	$ 111,122.60	$ 87,395.43	+L
15	$ 119,059.93	$ 92,649.53	+L
16	$ 126,997.26	$ 97,709.65	+L
17	$ 134,934.59	$ 102,531.78	+L
18	$ 142,871.92	$ 107,190.88	+L
19	$ 150,809.25	$ 111,580.83	+L
20	$ 158,746.58	$ 115,714.34	+L
21	$ 166,683.91	$ 119,572.87	+L
22	$ 174,624.23	$ 123,136.55	+L
23	$ 182,558.56	$ 126,684.05	+L
24	$ 190,495.89	$ 129,292.53	+L
25	$ 198,433.22	$ 131,837.47	+L
26	$ 206,370.55	$ 133,992.59	+L
27	$ 214,307.88	$ 135,729.71	+L
28	$ 222,245.21	$ 137,018.63	+L
29	$ 230,182.54	$ 137,826.93	+L
30	$ 238,119.87	$ 138,119.87	+L
	$ 238,119.87	$ 139,119.87	

APPRECIATION

YEAR	PROPERTY VALUE INCREASE
1	$ 5,000.00
2	$ 10,250.00
3	$ 15,762.50
4	$ 21,550.63
5	$ 27,628.16
6	$ 34,009.56
7	$ 40,710.04
8	$ 47,745.54
9	$ 55,132.82
10	$ 62,889.46
11	$ 71,033.94
12	$ 79,585.63
13	$ 88,564.91
14	$ 97,993.16
15	$ 107,892.82
16	$ 118,287.46
17	$ 129,201.83
18	$ 140,661.92
19	$ 152,695.02
20	$ 165,329.77
21	$ 178,596.26
22	$ 192,526.07
23	$ 207,152.38
24	$ 222,509.99
25	$ 238,635.49
26	$ 255,567.27
27	$ 273,345.63
28	$ 292,012.91
29	$ 311,613.56
30	$ 332,194.24
	$ 332,194.24

FIGURE 22: Cumulative Interest vs. Equity Buildup (I)

To the left (Figure 22) is the calculation using the Simple Leverage Loan Calculator. Note that the cumulative money paid is principal and interest, and in the next column you can see which portion is interest.

During the first year we paid $6,347 in interest from mortgage payments of $7,937. See fig. 23. The column on the left is both principal and interest, the column in the middle is the interest only, and the column on the right is the increase in the value of the property. We see (from the first line in the figure) that the value of the property has increased by $5,000 during the first year. However, we have paid $6,347.46 to earn that $5,000 in equity. In essence we lost $1,347.46 during the first year.

YEAR	CUMULATIVE MONEY PAID	CUMULATIVE INTEREST PAID	LEVERAGE	YEAR	PROPERTY VALUE INCREASE
1	$ 7.937.33	$ 6.347.46	–L	1	$ 5,000.00
2	$ 15,874.66	$ 13,201.86	–L	2	$ 10,250.00
3	$ 23,811.99	$ 19,977.98	–L	3	$ 15,762.50
4	$ 31,749.32	$ 26,670.16	–L	4	$ 21,550.63
5	$ 39,686.64	$ 33,272.32	–L	5	$ 27,628.16
6	$ 47,623.97	$ 39,777.96	–L	6	$ 34,009.56
7	$ 55,561.30	$ 46,180.11	–L	7	$ 40,710.04
8	$ 63,498.63	$ 52,471.27	–L	8	$ 47,745.54
9	$ 71,435.96	$ 58,643.44	–L	9	$ 55,132.82
10	$ 79,373.29	$ 64,688.00	–L	10	$ 62,889.46
11	$ 87,310.62	$ 70,595.74	+L	11	$ 71,033.94
12	$ 95,247.95	$ 76,356.75	+L	12	$ 79,585.63
13	$ 103,185.28	$ 81,960.44	+L	13	$ 88,564.91

FIGURE 23: CUMULATIVE INTEREST VS. EQUITY BUILDUP (II)

Now, look at the next year (line 2 above). We paid approximately $13,200 to create $10,250 in equity. So, again, we lost $2,950.

Starting at about the eleventh year (the third column), things switch over. The value of the property now is rising higher than the interest payments we're making. What we need to compare is the middle column interest amount versus the value of the property, not the total amount paid in the left-hand column.

In the eleventh year we paid a total interest of approximately $70,595 against a property that has now increased in value by $71,022. So we earned a little less than $1,000.

The reason we have to wait 11 years to see the point where our interest paid is working for us to create more equity is that we are using negative leverage. The interest rate is higher than the appreciation rate.

Property Value	$100,000.00
Amortized or Interest-Only	Fully Amortized
Loan Amount	$100,000.00
Number of Payments Per Year	12
Years	30
Interest	5.00%
Monthly Payment (P&I)	$534.59
Appreciation	5.00%
Mortgage Payments	$6,415.13
First Year Appreciation	$ 5,000.00

FIGURE 24: Example of Data Entered Into Calculator

If we change the numbers in Figure 24, i.e., use 5% for the interest rate for the loan (leverage) and maintain the projected appreciation rate of 5%, we can see on the chart below that the numbers have really gone up — to our benefit.

MORTGAGE PAYMENTS		APPRECIATION		
CUMULATIVE MONEY PAID	CUMULATIVE INTEREST PAID	LEVERAGE YEAR		PROPERTY VALUE INCREASE
1 $ 6,415.13	$ 4,530.95	+L 1		$ 5,000.00
2 $ 12,830.26	$ 9,401.67	+L 2		$ 10,250.00
3 $ 19,245.39	$ 14,193.37	+L 3		$ 15,762.50
4 $ 25,660.52	$ 18,902.01	+L 4		$ 21,550.63
5 $ 32,490.78	$ 23,523.35	+L 5		$ 27,628.16
6 $ 38,490.78	$ 28,052.91	+L 6		$ 34,009.56
7 $ 44,905.91	$ 32,486.01	+L 7		$ 40,710.04
8 $ 51,321.04	$ 36,817.70	+L 8		$ 47,745.54
9 $ 57,736.17	$ 41,042.79	+L 9		$ 55,132.82
10 $ 64,151.30	$ 45,155.84	+L 10		$ 62,889.46
11 $ 70,566.43	$ 49,151.12	+L 11		$ 71,033.94
12 $ 76,981.56	$ 53,022.58	+L 12		$ 79,585.63
13 $ 83,396.69	$ 56,763.91	+L 13		$ 88,564.91

FIGURE 25: Cumulative Interest vs. Equity Buildup (III)

What does that mean? Even though we're borrowing at 5% and the property is appreciating at 5%, the equity is growing exponentially. Over 30 years we've paid $92,000 in interest, but the property has generated equity of $332,000.

Let me draw that to your attention again. With a 5% interest rate and a 5% projected appreciation rate, we end up paying $92,000 in interest for an increase of $332,000. So, we are basically trading $92,000 for $332,000. The gain is more than $239,000!

As a result of positive leverage, during the first year we paid $4,530 in interest, but we made $5,000 in equity — a gain of $470. These are good examples of why we need to compare the interest and appreciation rates. These are the important bottom-line numbers.

If the appreciation rate is 8%, as it has been for the past 25 years in California, you'll notice that we pay $4,530 interest to create $8,000 in equity in the first year (using the same 5% interest for the leverage). Over time, we pay $92,000 in interest to generate $900,000 in equity (see Figure 26 below). We are earning a very powerful 1:10 ratio — another example of why we need to compare the interest rate and the appreciation rate.

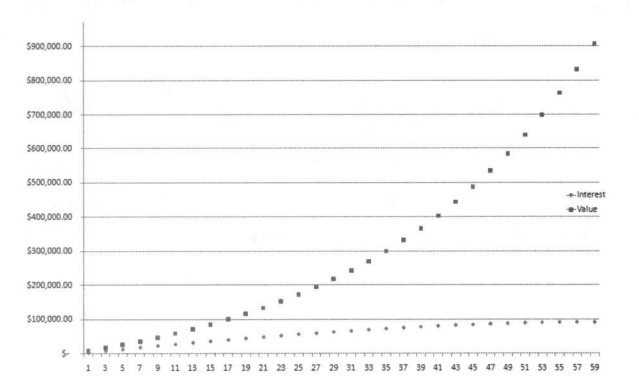

FIGURE 26: Cumulative Interest vs. Equity Buildup (IV)

When we look at the mortgage versus appreciation, we're not really comparing apples and apples. It's more like comparing apples and watermelons since we're borrowing at a fixed rate of interest and investing that money into a compounding investment, making great money. This is the best investment scenario you can get.

What you want to see is something like this:

Appreciation of 6% (compounding)

Interest Rate of 5% (fixed payments)

So even though it might appear that the spread above is 1%, it's actually a lot more, because the 6% is growing in a compounding manner while the 5% is fixed. The spread over time grows significantly. This is why real estate can be so amazing.

Let's reverse this. What if the appreciation is 5% and the interest rate is 8%? It takes 15 years to get positive leverage! Ideally, we want an interest rate lower than, or the same as, the appreciation.

For the ultimate leverage, look for the relationships in the box below:

> # Loan constant is less than cap rate.
> # Interest rate is less than appreciation rate.

Keep in mind that this allows for your cash flow and appreciation returns to be maximized. This kind of leverage also maximizes your equity, really in the Appreciation column, and can help if and when you choose to move to the Cash Flow column.

In summary, to maximize building equity, use leverage. Buy in traditionally appreciating areas. Also buy the right property types, such as single-family homes. Try to use an interest rate that is the same or lower than the projected appreciation rate. Be careful to keep an eye on the loan constant, because a higher loan constant is a higher-risk loan.

I'll offer more tips on maximizing for appreciation in Chapter 13.

"This is fabulous information. Wow!"

"Cash flow is great," my mentor acknowledged. "It covers your living expenses and any negative cash flow you might have from properties in the appreciation column. But know this one thing. . . ." My mentor leaned toward me, pointing his index finger in the air for emphasis. Whatever he was about to say was going to be extremely important. "The information I just shared with you about appreciation and leverage is what makes people very rich. Your equity can be used to buy much bigger cash flow properties. This is what you want to do so you can afford to go big. You go out and buy $10,000,000 of properties in an appreciating market with this kind of leverage — as long as your negative cash flow is covered or handled with positive cash flow from the Cash Flow column — and you will be set for life in a few years."

My mentor had given me a goal to strive for!

CHAPTER SUMMARY

- Appreciation compounds. This is a very important point.
- Compounding appreciation allows us to buy a property using leverage with fixed payments while the asset (property) grows in a compounding manner.
- Use the Simple Leverage Loan Calculator to figure out the numbers.
- It's ideal to borrow money at an interest rate less than or equal to the projected appreciation rate.
- You can still borrow money at an interest rate that's higher than the projected appreciation rate, but it will take a number of years to break even. Beyond that, though, it starts working for you.
- To maximize your appreciation return, buy in traditionally appreciating markets. Buy property types that have better appreciation, such as single-family homes. Condominiums and high-end homes do not perform as well, depending on the market.

CHAPTER SEVEN

Maximizing Both Cash Flow and Net Worth

"We're not done yet!"

"You mean it gets better?" I gasped!

"Sure. Hey, did you watch the football game last week?" asked my mentor seriously. He's a sports buff.

"Let me get this straight. You give me all this fabulous information, you get my heart really pumping, and then you ask me about sports?" I laughed. "Forget football. Tell me more."

IN THE PREVIOUS CHAPTER I EXPLAINED HOW TO USE LEVERAGE TO maximize appreciation. Now we have to start combining things. Whenever you buy a property, you need to look at how leverage affects cash flow *and* appreciation. Based on these two factors you can determine if you are comfortable moving forward on the purchase. You need to match those factors to your personal goals.

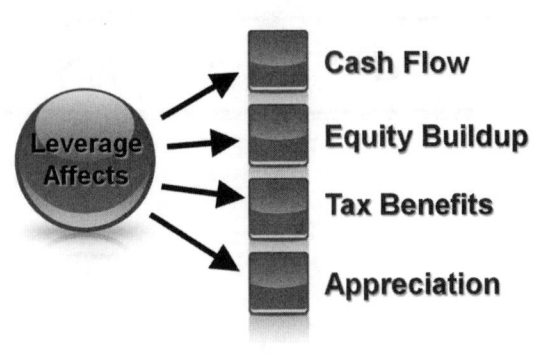

FIGURE 27: Leverage Affects All Profit Centers

In fact, you should really consider the effect of leverage on all four profit centers in real estate, as shown above.

Things to Consider

If you have negative leverage on your cash flow but positive leverage on your appreciation, are you willing to move forward with that? This could allow you to increase your net worth over time, but meanwhile you're dealing with negative leverage on the cash flow. Whether or not you do this depends on your goals.

If you're trying to maximize cash flow, this situation will not work. If your goal is longer-term appreciation, then this situation might be satisfactory. It all depends on what you're trying to do.

What if you have a situation with negative leverage on both your cash flow and your appreciation? Are you willing to move forward in this situation? Once again, it depends on your goals. I would consider this to be a bad deal because it wouldn't make my money work hard for me. So I wouldn't buy under these circumstances, but you may have a different motivation.

Most savvy investors would not do this, yet investors are doing exactly this today. They have no idea what they are doing!

What about the scenario of positive leverage on the cash flow and positive leverage on the appreciation? Are you willing to move forward with that? Is this a good situation?

Yes! Actually this is the ultimate leverage you want. This is exactly the type of deal you want to be involved in! This is how you maximize wealth.

As you go out looking at properties to buy, make sure they fit your criteria and match the leverage effects on the profit centers.

In certain areas of the United States, it might be more challenging to find positive leverage on both cash flow and appreciation. You have to buy way under market value or get the seller to finance you at an extremely low interest rate. So you need to be looking at these points of data and remember what you're trying to achieve.

Here's what you need to be looking for:

LEVERAGE	IS LESS THAN	PROPERTY
Loan Constant Rate	<	Capitalization Rate
Interest Rate	<	Capitalization Rate
Interest Rate	<	Projected Appreciation Rate

FIGURE 28: Conditions for Ultimate Leverage

You want the loan constant to be less than the cap rate and the interest rate to be less than the projected appreciation rate. This is what every savvy investor strives for. Yet, most investors I speak to these days have no clue what I'm talking about when I use these terms or talk about these concepts. It's extremely important that you know what you're looking for and that you start using leverage in the right way.

When I'm asked for specific examples of how to use these new tools, I direct students to two great vehicles for understanding and using leverage: apartment buildings and private lending. I'll suggest other vehicles in Chapter 12.

If you're not sure where to begin, pick cash flow. Savvy investors always start with cash flow first. Structure your investments (and leverage) to maximize cash flow.

"This is starting to make a lot more sense," I admitted. "Now, I have a good idea what to look for. You've simplified things for me quite a bit."

"Understanding leverage is one thing, George; doing it is another. And managing it is an entirely new thing," said my mentor as he stood up. "You should be drinking more water, George. It's good for you," he added as he headed toward the water cooler.

CHAPTER SUMMARY

- Make sure that deals fit your criteria, and match the leverage effects on the profit centers to your goals.
- You can choose leverage that maximizes cash flow over appreciation; you can also choose the opposite. And, with the right kind of leverage, you can maximize both cash flow and appreciation.
- If you're not sure where to begin, start with cash flow. Savvy investors start by generating cash flow first.
- The perfect leverage is when the loan constant is less than the cap rate and the interest rate is less than the projected appreciation rate.

CHAPTER EIGHT

Managing Risk

"So, what do I mean by managing leverage?" my mentor asked as he handed me a cup of cold water.

"Well, you mentioned that leverage has risk. Leverage can work both ways. It can make you wealthy, but it can also hurt you. I now understand that negative leverage can hurt people if they're not careful. Positive leverage can help people become wealthy."

"Right," he affirmed, "but when I say 'managing leverage,' I'm referring to managing the risk of leverage."

"So how does one manage the risk associated with leverage?"

MANY "EXPERTS" WILL SAY THAT LEVERAGE IS A TOTALLY SAFE WAY TO build wealth. Not true!

This chapter is about the risk — and the management of that risk — associated with using leverage. There is a big difference between "risky" and "managing risk," as we will find out. I'm *not* saying that investing in real estate is inherently risky. In fact, real estate is one of the safer investments, especially when compared to the stock market. We're now going to look at how to measure and control risk.

> For the savvy, building wealth is not risky.
> It's not risky because they invest
> and manage risk.

There's a big difference in taking risks and managing risk associated with an investment. Knowledgeable wealth builders understand risk, quantify it, hedge against it, and have contingency plans in place because of it. I once heard an experienced wealth builder say it best: "Cover the downside and let the upside take care of itself."

The worksheet below is one I normally use in identifying risks. Use of this worksheet is beyond the scope of this book; however, I explain how to use it in more detail in The Wealthy Code Inner Circle, a membership community seeking to become wealthy. (Please refer to the Resources section.)

RISK	RISK MITIGATION	CONTINGENCY PLAN
Investor Dies	N/A	Buy life insurance to cover all money partners

FIGURE 29: Risk-Planning Worksheet

Who is at greater risk of getting hurt?

Figure 30: Understanding Risk

Understanding Risk

Imagine two people standing on narrow, round platforms, as shown in Figure 30. The platform on the left shows the person balancing about 8 feet off the ground; the platform on the right shows the person standing only about 2 feet off the ground. Which of these two people is at greater "risk" of getting hurt?

The potential for injury is greater for the one on the left, on the higher platform, since that individual has farther to fall. When we substitute leverage for the pillars, we realize that the person with greater leverage has more financial risk; conversely, the person with less leverage has less financial risk. So the more leverage you add to a deal, the higher the platform goes; the less the leverage, the lower the platform.

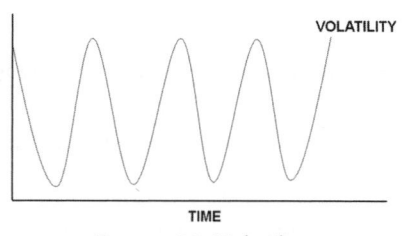

FIGURE 31: Volatility

When we talk about risk we need to talk about volatility. Volatility is also referred to as the Standard Deviation. (See definition below.) Think of a chart, perhaps of the stock market, showing a great deal of up and down movement over time. This is volatility.

STANDARD DEVIATION

"Standard deviation is a widely used measure of variability or dispersion. ... It shows how much variation there is from the 'average' (mean). A low standard deviation indicates that the data points tend to be very close to the mean, whereas high standard deviation indicates that the data are spread out over a large range of values." – Wikipedia.org

---

FIGURE 32: Definition of Standard Deviation

When there is less change from the "average" line, the action or movement is less volatile. For an illustration of low volatility, envision small ripples in a swimming pool. For high volatility, think of waves in the North Atlantic in winter — or a stock market price chart over the past two or three years! There is certainly less risk involved with a low-volatility asset, but the returns are also smaller. On the other hand, there is more risk with a higher volatility, but the chance for bigger returns is greater.

> ## "Volatility" refers to the amount of uncertainty or risk about the size of changes in a security's value.
> ### – INVESTOPEDIA.COM

The greater change there is (up and down on the chart) the greater the risk.

> ## More leverage can lead to higher returns (if positive leverage).
> ## More leverage also leads to more volatility.
> ## More volatility leads to more risk.
> ## More volatility also leads to more fluctuation in cash flow.
> ## More fluctuation in cash flow leads to more fluctuation in returns.

This is the effect of leverage.

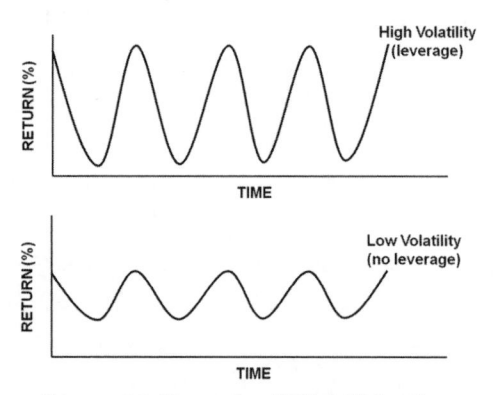

FIGURE 33: Example of High Volatility

Volatility fluctuates, depending on a number of factors. For example, leverage magnifies returns, which creates more volatility in our returns. Another factor affecting volatility is the nature of the investment. Some investments, such as the stock market, are inherently volatile, while others, like real estate, are more stable.

When looking at volatility, we need to separate the "value" of an asset from the "income" that asset produces. Let's start with the latter.

Volatility and an Asset's Income

Consider the income produced by an asset. Let's use the cap rate as a measure of the income here and assume the value of the asset is stable. Leverage has no effect on the income of an asset or on the cap rate. Leverage does, however, have an impact on the *returns* for the investor.

As mentioned earlier, leverage with a low loan constant results in a much higher return (due to a bigger spread with the cap rate). If the leverage has a higher loan constant, the return is much lower (due to a lower spread with the cap rate). Also, the greater the leverage (the more borrowed money we have in a deal) the higher the return fluctuates. Consider this example.

Maria buys an apartment building for $200,000 all cash, meaning no leverage was used (see Figure 34). It is fully occupied, and she receives $30k per year in passive income from that investment. After paying the $14k of operating expenses, she is left with $16k for the year. Since she used all cash for the purchase, she doesn't have to worry about paying a lender. Assume her gross income drops by 20% (perhaps her tenants move out); she will receive $24k instead of $30k. After paying her $14k of operating expenses, she will still be left with $10k ($24k - $14k) and will also have positive cash flow. Her return fluctuated a little: at 100% occupancy she made an 8% return ($16k/$200k), while with an 80% occupancy, she made a 5% return ($10k/$200k).

DESCRIPTION	MARIA		PABLO	
	100% OCCUPANCY	80% OCCUPANCY	100% OCCUPANCY	80% OCCUPANCY
Price of Building	$200,000	$200,000	$200,000	$200,000
Down Payment	$200,000	$200,000	$ 40,000	$ 40,000
Gross Potential Income	$ 30,000	$ 30,000	$ 30,000	$ 30,000
Occupancy	100%	80%	100%	80%
Effective Gross Income *minus* Oper. Expenses	$ 30,000 −$ 14,000	$ 24,000 −$ 14,000	$ 30,000 −$ 14,000	$ 24,000 −$ 14,000
Net Operating Income	$ 16,000	$ 10,000	$ 16,000	$ 10,000
Debt Service (mortgage)	$ −	$ −	−$ 10,307	−$ 10,307
Cash Flow	$ 16,000	$ 10,000	$ 5,693	$ (307)
Cash-on-Cash Return	8.00%	5.00%	14.230%	−.077%

FIGURE 34: Maria and Pablo's Returns

On the other hand, Pablo purchased exactly the same property next door for the same price of $200,000. It too is fully occupied. He used leverage (borrowed money) to buy this property by borrowing 80% of the price ($160,000). He used his own cash of $40,000 as down payment. His annual mortgage payments are $10,307, and he collects his

$30k per year in income. He pays his operating expenses of $14k (which does not include his mortgage payment) along with his mortgage payment of $10,307. He is now left with $5,693 in cash flow for the year. If we assume the same 20% drop in his gross income, he will receive $24k. He has to pay his operating expenses of $14k and his mortgage payments of $10,307 (also known as debt service). He will then have to pay $307 out of his pocket and now ends up with negative cash flow. His return fluctuated quite a bit more than Maria's. At 100% occupancy, he made a 14.23% return ($5693/$40k), while at 80% occupancy, he had a -0.77 % return (-$307/$40k).

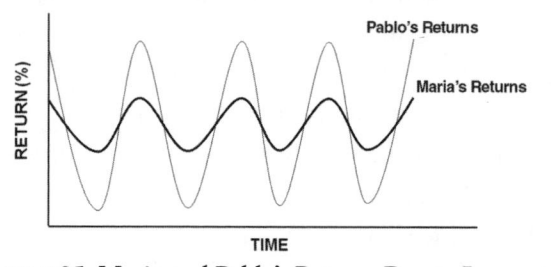

FIGURE 35: Maria and Pablo's Returns Due to Leverage

These examples illustrate how the returns changed based on the leverage. The figure above shows the volatility of the returns. Remember that it was the same building, same cap rate, same conditions. The only change between both deals is the introduction of leverage. The return was lower for Maria's building without leverage along with lower volatility. Maria's returns in the example fluctuated between 8% and 5%. Pablo's deal had a higher return with leverage as well as higher volatility. When the income dropped, it had a magnified effect on the returns due to leverage. So the returns have been magnified with leverage, resulting in higher fluctuation or volatility. Pablo's returns in the example fluctuated between 14.23% and -0.77% for the same drop in income as Maria's.

This might frighten some people, and their first reaction is "I should just buy everything with cash and with no leverage." But that isn't the case. You have to realize that with leverage you can buy an asset without having to provide all the money. Furthermore, I'll explain how to manage risk and shift some of the risk away from you. Maria could have purchased four more properties for the same money she used to purchase this property and ended up with a lot more cash in her pocket. Also, her net worth from appreciation would increase many times faster than it would have if she had owned just one building, as we shall find out in a little bit.

So, in summary, leverage magnifies returns, which in turn magnifies volatility. That in turn reflects an increase in risk.

Volatility and an Asset's Value

The nature of investment vehicles also has to do with volatility. For example, a frequently traded investment vehicle, such as the stock market, is normally highly volatile. Real estate is an investment of low volatility and is a much more stable investment. That means less risk. Over the 10-year period of 1998 to 2007 the standard deviation (measure of volatility) of real estate was 1.3%. Compare that to the 10.3% standard deviation of the S&P 500 over the same period. This illustrates the stability of real estate over time, as compared to the highly volatile stock market. Furthermore, the tenants are paying off your mortgage, and you don't have to sell in a panic as you would with the stock market.

When real estate "crashes" 15%, most people panic, but fluctuations of this magnitude can happen almost any day in the stock market. Many people don't recognize real estate for the safe, low volatility investment that it is.

Adding leverage to an already volatile investment vehicle introduces additional volatility, which in turn increases risk. For example, if you use 50% of borrowed money (along with your own cash for the remaining 50%) to buy a stock, given that stocks are volatile to begin with, you effectively doubled the volatility of the returns on that stock.

I'm talking specifically about the value of the asset, not the income. As mentioned in Chapter 2, the wealthy start by making sure they have "cash flow" investments in their portfolio, followed by "capital gains" investments. In this section I'm focusing on the "capital gains" investments — the ones you buy and then pray will go up in value over time to sell.

Let's consider an example. Say that you buy a property for $100,000 all cash, and you own the property free and clear. In the first year the market rises 8% with an appreciation of $8,000. Because you invested $100,000 you made an 8% return on your money (from the appreciation alone).

What would have happened if you had bought the same property for $100,000, all cash, and the property depreciated by 8%? You would have lost $8,000 in equity over your investment of $100,000. That's also 8%.

Now, let's say that you buy the same $100,000 property, putting $20,000 down. This is a 1:5 leverage because you're investing out-of-pocket only one-fifth (20%) of the value of the property. When the market goes up, as in the first example above, you've made $8,000 in equity, but you invested $20,000 cash, so you made a 40% return on your money (we're looking at equity alone in this example).

Of course, using the same example, when the market goes down 8% you've lost $8,000 in equity. You invested $20,000, and so now you've lost 40%. That was for a 5:1 leverage.

Notice the leverage on the left-hand side of the table below. Notice the range of gain and loss on the right-hand side. With more leverage, you have a wider range of profit or loss, which goes back to "more leverage = more fluctuations = more risk."

LEVERAGE BY INVESTMENT	RANGE OF RISK
All Cash	−8% to 8%
5:1 leverage (20% down)	−40% to +40%
3:1 leverage (33% down)	−24% to +24%
X:1 leverage (unknown $ down)	−8X% to +8X%
What if no $ out-of-pocket?	Unlimited loss or profit

FIGURE 36: Showing Range of Risk

Consider the table above from the example we're using. Notice that higher leverage creates higher risk.

So in summary, leverage magnifies returns, which in turn magnifies volatility. That in turn reflects an increase in risk. The goal is to find a stable asset that appreciates steadily over time with little volatility and that has consistent income stream.

In the Simple Leverage Loan Calculator output (below), look at the listing on the left for an entry titled "Leverage Ratio." When there's a 1 in that row, it means you bought something all cash. That makes it safe but with limited returns.

6 Primary Financing				
Loan LTV ....%		80%	80%	80%
Loan Amount ....OR $		0	0	0
Loan Amount Used (L)		$ 80,000	$ 80,000	$ 80,000
Amortized or Interest-Only.................		Fully Amortizing	Fully Amortizing	Interest Only
Interest Rate		5.00%	7.00%	5.00%
Term (years)...		30	30	30
Periods Per Year		12	12	12
Monthly Payments....................$0.00		$429.46	$532.24	$333.33
Annual Payments.......................$0.00		$5,153.49	$6,386.90	$4,000.00
Loan Constant......................................		6.44%	7.96%	5.00%
7 Leverage Ratio (V/E)	1	5	5	5

FIGURE 37: The Simple Leverage Loan Calculator Output

Notice in the image above that the last line shows the leverage ratio described earlier. The line before that shows the loan constant of the financing as entered by the user (in the gray areas). Notice the 5s in the Leverage Ratio columns. That indicates 5:1 leverage, meaning 80% loan and 20% cash invested.

How can you cover the downside?

So, is leverage "risky"? No, but you do need to manage it.

There are methods to cover the downside. For instance, when higher leverage creates volatility, getting equity partners can lower your return (covered in more detail in Chapter 9), but it also helps to cover the downside and the volatility. While many investors look at only the upside, savvy ones cover the downside. Savvy investors measure the upside and cover the downside.

Overall, real estate has a low standard deviation, meaning that it is very stable and, therefore, can be safe. Knowledgeable investors can get 20% to 80% total returns while hedging against the downside, just by knowing the possibilities.

Spread Risk

Remember that cash flow comes from spreads, or arbitrage, and arbitrage is a leveraged strategy. Anytime you talk about spreads, especially when you have small spreads, make sure you control both ends of the spread: the loan constant and the performance of the asset (the cap rate).

For example, if you purchased an asset that generates an 8% cap rate while the loan constant pays 7%, and any of those numbers fluctuate (such as the loan constant becoming higher than the cap rate or the cap rate becoming less than the loan constant), you end up with negative leverage.

Controlling both ends of the spread becomes important, and both ends of the spread are important risks to control. Here is a simple way to control the risk. Make sure you minimize volatility on both ends. That means you want to have little or no fluctuation on either end.

In a perfect world, both the loan constant and the cap rate will be fixed for 30 years. This guarantees your spread for 30 years. But, alas, not everything is that perfect.

So what do you do? Here are a few things to consider.

• Make sure the loan constant is either fixed (by getting a fixed-rate loan) or based on a stable index, such as the London Interbank Offered Rate – LIBOR. The LIBOR is a daily reference rate based on the interest rates at which banks borrow unsecured funds from other banks in the London wholesale money market. This is important because it is also the rate upon which rates for many other borrowers are based.

Basically, anytime you can get a fixed-interest-rate loan, get it. If you can only get a variable-interest loan, get one that adjusts less frequently (maybe once a year) and is based on a stable, minimal-fluctuation index. This allows you to control one end of the spread.

- To control the other end, the cap rate, make sure the asset you're buying is also stable or has minimal volatility. I pointed out earlier that real estate is not a volatile asset. However, even within real estate, there are factors that can make it more or less volatile. Understanding these factors becomes very important. Here are a few tips to keep the cap rate stable:

  - The more units, the better. For example, in a single-family home, if a tenant moves out you have 100% vacancy and no income. That makes your cap rate drop! In a 100-unit building, if 1 person leaves, you have 99 other occupied units. So the more units there are, the more stable the cap rate.

  - A bigger spread is better than a smaller spread. That gives you more "cushion" to absorb greater volatility. The wider the spread, the higher the cash-on-cash return and the better able you are to absorb the volatility. The smaller the spread, the lower the cash-on-cash return and the less able you are to absorb the volatility.

  - Make a larger down payment (which affects returns negatively but which gives you a more stable building). A bigger down payment means less leverage.

  - Good management keeps vacancy low and a stable cap rate.

  - Buy in a stable area and job market with diverse industries, along with a larger population.

  - For others assets, a stable history of performance (for the past 25 yrs.).

  - Structuring better OPM. Should you borrow the down payment or invite people to be equity partners? How does this affect risk? I'll explain this in more detail in the next chapter.

Measuring Another Important Spread

The spread I've been mentioning so far is the cap rate and the loan constant. There is another corresponding spread: the difference between the net operating income (NOI) and the annual debt service (the annual loan payment).

Property Price =	$100,000
Income	$ 10,000
– Expenses	$ 4,000
= Net Operating Income (NOI)	$ 6,000
– Mortgage	$ 4,000
Cash Flow	$ 2,000
CapRate = NOI/Price = $6k/$100k = 6%	

FIGURE 38: Sample Calculation

Consider the calculations above. The spread between the NOI and the annual debt service (shown as Mortgage above) is as follows:

$$\text{Spread = NOI – mortgage payment =}$$
$$\$6,000 – \$4,000 = \$2,000$$

This tells us that we're making $2,000 more than we're paying the lender. This is the spread, or cushion, we have. So if the income fluctuates, we can afford up to $2,000 in fluctuations to cover the lender's payment.

However, a better way is to calculate this as a percentage of how much more money we're making than we're paying the lender. Let's call that the "cushion" for now. A more helpful way is to do the following:

$$\text{Cushion = NOI/Mortgage payments}$$
$$\text{Cushion = } \$6,000/\$4,000$$
$$\text{Cushion = 1.50}$$

What does the 1.50 mean? Let's start with the term "cushion." The correct term is Debt Coverage Ratio (DCR). So let's figure out what this number means.

DCR = 1.50

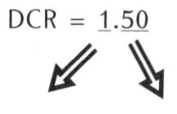

1 or 100%	.50 or 50%
Mortgage Payment	Amount in YOUR Pocket

FIGURE 39: Understanding DCR

Refer to the diagram above. The 1 in the 1.50 is the money that goes to the lender. This is the mortgage payment. Any number higher than 1 is the portion that goes into your pocket and is a measure of how much more money you're keeping than what you're paying the lender. So, in our example, the 50 in 1.50 means we're making 50% more money than what we're paying the lender.

The DCR must exceed 1.0 for the asset to make the mortgage payment.

A DCR of 1.20 means we're making 20% more than what we're paying the lender. This corresponds to the spread between cap rate and the loan constant but isn't the same.

A DCR of 0.75 means we're losing money. The asset isn't generating enough money to make the mortgage payment. The asset is covering only 75% of the mortgage payment. We have to come out of pocket (the remaining 25%) to cover the mortgage payment.

So, essentially, when we talk about a wider spread, we're talking about the DCR being a higher number.

The higher the DCR, the higher the spread and the more volatility we can absorb. A DCR of 1.40 is better than 1.10. This tells us there's a 40% cushion and a wider spread; 1.10 tells us there's a 10% spread (or cushion).

A comfortable DCR we should aim for varies with the volatility of the asset. A highly volatile investment requires a higher DCR. In real

Debt Coverage Ratio is a measure of
the spread between NOI and debt service
(loan payments). It tells us how much more
money we keep than we pay the lender.
We refer to it as the "cushion."

DCR = NOI/Loan payments

estate, due to its lower volatility, a DCR of 1.20 is considered a good minimum to aim for. That means we would be comfortable with a spread of 20%. This is how much more money we should keep than what we pay the lender, the cushion we should aim for.

The Simple Leverage Loan Calculator
calculates the DCR for you.

You might wonder if the spread between the NOI and the mortgage payments replaces the previous spread of the cap rate and the loan constant. It does not. The cap rate and the loan constant spread tell us if something is positive, neutral, or negative leverage. The NOI and the mortgage payments spread tell us if we have positive or negative cash flow. There is a big difference. This is where more than 95% of investors fail!

You can have positive cash flow with negative leverage (due to a big down payment). And you can have neutral leverage and still have positive cash flow. You really need to consider both spreads.

"So, cover the downside and let the upside take care of itself."

"Exactly, George," responded my mentor. "Being wealthy is about creating cash flow from spreads by using leverage while covering the downside. Savvy wealth builders understand the difference between something being risky and managing risk. They also know how to lower risk."

CHAPTER SUMMARY

- Risk is tied to volatility. The higher the volatility, the higher the risk. The lower the volatility, the lower the risk.

- In many cases, the standard deviation is used to define volatility. So, once again, the higher the standard deviation, the higher the risk, and vice versa.

- Leverage increases potential returns, but it also increases volatility, which in turn increases risk.

- Leverage also increases potential losses because of the same increase in volatility and risk.

- An investment being risky is not the same as managing the risk of an investment. Savvy wealth builders manage risk, but they are not being risky.

- Debt Coverage Ratio (DCR) is a measure of the spread between NOI and debt service (loan payments). The DCR tells us how much more money we keep than we pay the lender. We refer to it as the cushion.

- With a DCR of 1.30, for instance, the 1 in 1.30 is the money that goes to the lender; the .30 is the 30% more that goes into our pocket than what we pay the lender.

- A "comfortable" DCR we should aim for varies depending on the volatility of the asset. A minimum DCR to aim for in real estate is 1.20.

CHAPTER NINE

Structuring Safer Down Payments

"So I understand leverage, and I know how to calculate it. I get how to identify the right properties and match them with the right leverage. I know how to manage risk," I declared. "But what about getting the down payment to buy these assets in the first place? How do I structure that?"

"Great questions!" My mentor's tone became more serious. "This is very important, George. Structuring this wrong can be devastating, but structuring it right can be very profitable."

IN THE PREVIOUS CHAPTERS I'VE EMPHASIZED THE IMPORTANCE OF using positive leverage. I've also focused on the importance of managing risk. (I'm working my way down the list of items you need to have in place to become wealthy and, ultimately, get out of the rat race.) I've also shown how positive leverage leads to higher cash-on-cash return, while negative leverage leads to lower cash-on-cash return. In Chapter 4, I explained how to calculate the cash-on-cash return. We'll be using that calculation in this chapter.

The Two Parts of Buying an Asset

In most cases, you'll need to have a down payment to buy an asset. The purchase of an asset typically has two parts: the "finance stack" and the down payment.

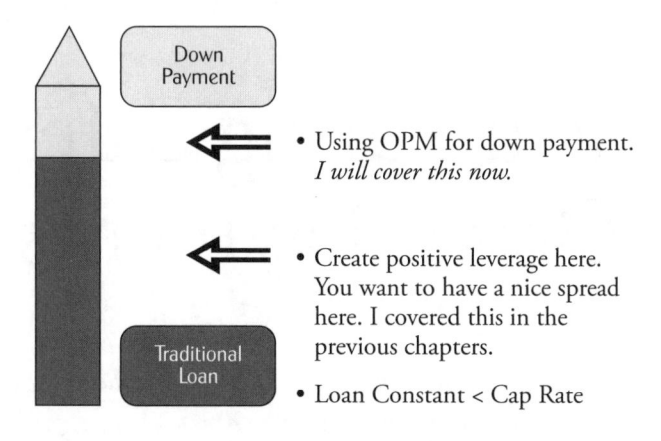

FIGURE 40: Two Parts of Buying an Asset

The "finance stack" is the combination of all the financing (or leverage) you're using to cover most of the purchase, such as a mortgage. Everything I have covered so far about leverage applies to this portion. It's the biggest portion of the money needed to buy an asset.

The down payment is money required by the lender to buy the asset. This chapter will cover what you need to know about the down payment. Please read this carefully because the rules for the down payment are different from the rules of the "finance stack."

Down Payment

I'm going to assume that you'll be raising capital (using OPM) for the down payment. The question you have to ask yourself is, "What is the best way to structure OPM for the down payment?"

There are three basic possibilities for structuring OPM:
• Debt financing

• Equity financing

• Combination

Debt financing is when you borrow money from someone and agree to pay them a certain interest rate on their money. For example, "James, I'll borrow $20,000 from you at 10% for 5 years. I'll pay you $166.67 per month for 5 years, and then at the end of the 5 years I'll pay you the balance." This is an example of debt financing where you're borrowing money at a certain interest rate. Their reward for lending their money is the interest rate.

Equity financing is when someone lends you the money you do not have to pay until the conclusion of the deal, when they get part of the profit. This in reality is not lending but investing. "James, for your $20,000 investment, I'll pay you 50% of the profit. When I sell the property, I'll pay you back your $20,000, and then we'll split the profits 50/50 above and beyond that." Notice that this is not borrowing money. The other party is investing their money. The reward for use of their money is a percentage of the profit.

Combination is simply a combination of the first two. I won't deal with the combination approach in this book.

So which is best to use: debt financing or equity financing? In other words, should we *borrow* the money from someone at an agreed-upon interest rate, or should we have that person *invest* his money in exchange for a percentage of the profit?

Safer Structure

In general, whenever you're raising capital for new projects, offering equity rather than debt financing is safer for you. The investor putting up the capital shares in the upside — and the downside — of the project.

As I explained in the previous chapter, the more leverage you have, the more volatility you incur and, as a result, the more risk. So by using debt financing for the down payment, you're increasing volatility and, therefore, risk.

> **If you use debt financing for the down payment, you increase volatility and risk.**
>
> **If you use equity financing for the down payment, you choose the safer and more stable route.**

So choose equity financing for a less volatile and, therefore, safer deal.

How Much Do I Give Up For OPM?

A very common question I get is, "How much should I pay someone who invests their capital as down payment?" The rule of thumb is as follows:

Step 1: Calculate your cash-on-cash return for the down payment.

Step 2: For equity financing, give 50% or less.

Step 3: For debt financing, borrow money at a lower rate (preferably 50% or less) than the cash-on-cash return.

Let me expand on these with an example.

If your cash-on-cash return on the down payment is 16% and you offer 50% of the cash flow, you're essentially giving them 50% of the cash-on-cash return. So, in this example, they receive 8% cash-on-cash return on their money. They also share in the upside and the downside of all four profit centers, not just cash flow.

Suppose your down payment requirement was $50,000. An investor looking for cash flow agrees to invest the entire $50,000. You calculate that the cash-on-cash return is 14%; you then restructure the leverage to create a bigger spread. Your cash-on-cash return now goes up to 15%.

You offer the investor the option of a 50/50 split or 12% on his $50,000. He chooses the 50/50 split. Well, he ends up getting 50% of the 15% cash-on-cash, which is 7.5% cash-on-cash return! So he actually makes a lot less than the latter option of the 12% (at least for now). Also, if the cash-on-cash goes down to 5%, he simply makes half of that! On the other hand, over time, as the cash flow and the equity increase, he shares in the upside of the property.

If he had selected debt financing, you would have incurred more risk. First you increased your leverage, which increased volatility and risk. He takes 12% of the 15% cash-on-cash, which keeps a 3% spread for you. The minute your asset starts underperforming, everything now turns to negative leverage. However, in the long run, you don't have to share in the upside.

Savvy investors cover the downside and let the upside take care of itself. With that in mind, savvy wealth builders raise capital by offering equity in the deal. This allows for a much more stable asset while covering the downside. The upside will take care of itself.

Typical Mistakes

I've seen wealth builders offer OPM sources 12% on their money when the property's cash-on-cash is 12%. That means they end up with $0 coming in while maximizing volatility and risk in the deal!

I've also heard some gurus out there telling individuals to use credit card cash advances as a down payment. The cash-on-cash might be 12%. Cash advance rates are probably north of 24%! In that case, they end up with maximum leverage, maximum volatility, and too much risk.

The list goes on and on. These mistakes are due to a lack of education. It's become a lot more common to find investors who buy with negative leverage, borrowing their down payment source as debt financing and paying a rate that exceeds the cash-on-cash rate! No wonder so many investors are losing their shirts!

To summarize, when raising capital for down payment, remember this: Getting equity partners allows for a more stable building. You keep the volatility under control. Your equity partners act as the cushion. And borrowing the down payment adds more volatility to the deal.

"Dude, my mind is fried!" I stood up and walked to the window. I looked out at the parking lot, which was full of cars. All these people are paying my mentor monthly checks — rent. "What's amazing," I said, "is that you don't just understand this, you do it. You used that information to transform your life. This is great!"

"It wasn't easy," my mentor observed as he turned toward his desktop computer to check his e-mail. "Wealthy people earn their stripes. It's the way the universe tests you, to make sure you're absolutely committed to doing whatever you're trying to do, and that you earn it. I've been broke and I've been rich, and I can tell you I prefer rich. Most people that try one thing and fail give up too easily. They justify it by saying, 'This doesn't work!' Do you know whose loss it is, George, when they do that?" my mentor asked.

"Theirs, of course," I answered.

"Yes, it is theirs. But it's also a loss to their family, their friends, the next generation, and most important, every person they would have helped. Do you see how many people that might be? One decision of giving up has a huge effect on many people's lives. Unfortunately, most people give up too easily!" he said, shaking his head sadly.

"So true," I replied. For a minute there, I was reminded of my late father. He loved educating me and my brothers (when we were willing to listen) about business and the importance of never giving up.

As my mentor spoke, I was transported back in time. It was the evening of August 8th, 1987. My father and I had had a very busy day. My mother and two younger brothers were on vacation, and my father and I had agreed to stay back and run the family businesses, including a restaurant, a guest inn, a construction company, an insurance agency, and some real estate, among other things.

It was a clear evening as my father and I stood in front of our restaurant. He was sharing with me his plans for the coming months and year. I had been working with him for the previous two-and-a-half years while I went to school. That evening, I had felt he was indirectly telling me — 18 at the time — I was ready to take on a bigger role.

Little did I know that the next day would be the last day of his life. He passed away on August 9th, 1987, and our lives were changed in an instant. Three young boys — 18, 17, and 15 years old, along with my mother — were devastated.

The sudden ringing of the phone interrupted my memories.

CHAPTER SUMMARY

- Step 1: Calculate your cash-on-cash return for the down payment.
- Step 2: For equity financing, give 50% or less.
- Step 3: For debt financing, borrow money at a lower rate than the cash-on-cash return.
- For down payment, always go with equity financing, not debt financing.
- Get comfortable calculating your — and the investors' — portion of the cash flow when raising debt or equity financing.

CHAPTER TEN

The "Best" Leverage

"Let me take this call," my mentor said as he picked up the receiver. "It'll just take a second."

I stepped out of the office to give him some privacy.

After only few minutes, he walked out of his office chuckling.

"That was my wife's friend asking me what the best mortgage would be. People think I can point them to one loan and say, 'Get that.' You see, George, everyone out there needs this information."

"Actually, let me put you on the spot," I said, a little hesitantly. "What would you say if I asked, 'What is the best leverage?'"

"Well, where do I start? It really depends on what you're trying to do."

AT THIS POINT I'M GOING TO BEGIN CHALLENGING MANY WIDELY HELD beliefs. I'll integrate some of the strategies mentioned earlier and introduce some new concepts.

In fact, the content in this chapter has been the subject of heated debates with some of my students because of their mindsets. The best debates were with real estate agents who had absolutely believed that what I am about to share with you is "bad advice" — until I walked them through the details.

It was an eye-opening experience for them.

I'll be explaining how to optimize mortgages (leverage) on any property or asset, how to get the best positive leverage using your equity, and suggesting some tools you can use. This information builds on previous chapters.

There are many aspects to mortgages. You probably know about some of them, but in this chapter I'm going to be covering a few that aren't normally described. Home ownership is one of the largest investments you will ever make, so you need to know how to do it right.

Let's Start From the Beginning

Between these two opportunities, which would you pick?
1. A risky loan with a low interest rate
2. A less-risky loan with a slightly higher interest rate

Take a minute to seriously think about this and make your choice.

Savvy investors choose the less-risky loan with the slightly higher interest rate. Unfortunately, most people end up choosing the riskier loan out of ignorance. They are jeopardizing their wealth by doing that.

I have a couple of goals in this section. I want you to know why choosing opportunity number 2, above, is better and how to determine that for yourself. I also want to show you how to generate more wealth by simply maximizing the use of your equity in your real estate while minimizing risk. Most people use the equity without even thinking about minimizing the risk.

In subsequent sections, I'll refer back to the question posed above. What is this investment?

- You deposit a one-time payment.

- Money is locked up for a predetermined time that you pick.

- If you withdraw money early, you're penalized.

- Money is not liquid.

- Money is safe and secured by FDIC.

- You get interest payments during that period.

So what is this investment?

If you said a CD, you're right. The investment described above is a bank Certificate of Deposit.

Do you think *this* is a good investment?

- You pick the monthly payments you make.
- If you pay less than the amount you pick, you could lose all the previous payments made.
- Each payment makes the money you have paid less safe.
- Money is not liquid; nor is it safe.
- The money earns *zero* percent return!

Is this a good investment?

Most people are already "invested" in this. It's their house!

Equity in a house is a bad investment. It sits there and does nothing for the homeowner.

> **Equity in a house is a bad investment.**
> **It sits there and does nothing for you.**

We need to learn to turn "dead" equity in our houses into cash for us!

Here's what this chapter covers:

1. How much mortgage (leverage) should I have?
2. Return on equity
3. Which mortgage (leverage) is best to have?
4. Better way to pay off the mortgage (leverage)
5. Turning leverage equity into wealth
6. Resources

How Much Mortgage Should I Have?

Assume the scenario below:

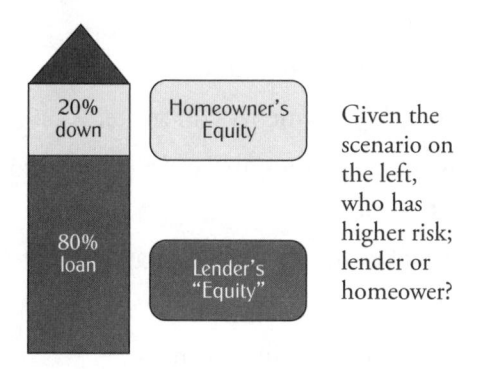

FIGURE 41: Who's Taking The Higher Risk?

A homeowner gets a loan for 80% of a property, making a down payment of 20%. Whose money is at a higher risk? The homeowner's or the lender's?

The homeowner's money is at a higher risk because if they need to sell the property — with the commission and closing costs and all fees involved with doing that — they will lose part of their down payment, and the lender gets back their full 80% loan money. The homeowner's money goes first, before the lender's money is affected.

So the lender was in the safer position; the homeowner took the higher risk.

Now, consider the scenario in Figure 42.

Between the two deals shown, (same property) — the lender lends a 90% loan and the homeowner puts 10% down, *or* the lender lends a 70% loan and the homeowner pays 30% down — which is safer for the lender?

Would the lender be in a better position with a larger loan or a smaller loan?

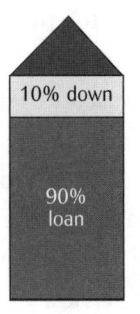
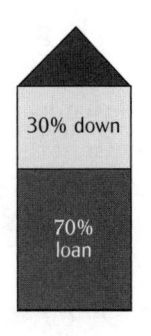

10% down

90% loan

Which of these two deals is safer for the lender, left or right?

30% down

70% loan

FIGURE 42: Which Scenario Is Safer For The Lender?

The answer is, the lender prefers the right-hand deal — lending less money.

The lender in the latter position has more cushion if the property value goes up or down. The lender is better off lending a smaller amount toward the full price of the property. By doing that, the lender shifts the risk towards the homeowner.

The former deal, where the homeowner paid only 10% down, is better for the homeowner, having less to lose. By doing that, the homeowner shifted risk toward the lender (even though the homeowner is still in a riskier position, but the homeowner shifted some towards the lender).

Now, consider this scenario below.

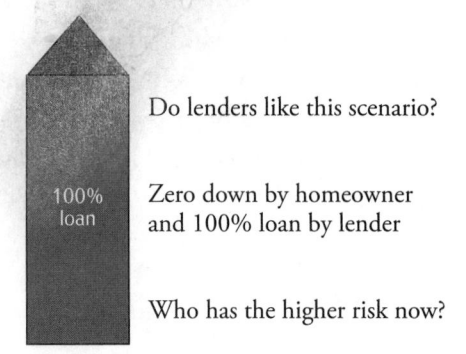

Do lenders like this scenario?

100% loan

Zero down by homeowner and 100% loan by lender

Who has the higher risk now?

FIGURE 43: Is This a Favorable Position For The Lender?

Do lenders like putting up 100% of the loan with the homeowner putting nothing down? What happens if the homeowner walks away from this? The lender takes all the risk. So in this case, the lender shifted the risk away from the homeowner.

This is the scenario that happened in the late 2000s and is why the lenders got into trouble. They shifted the risk away from the homeowners and towards themselves. So, since they shared little or no risk, many homeowners simply walked away from their properties.

Take a look at the scenario below.

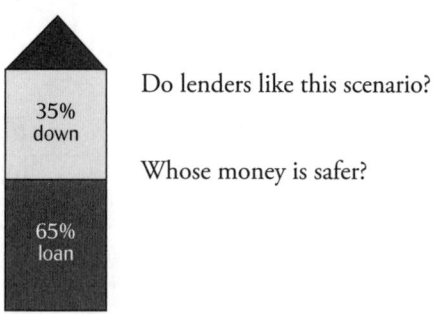

Do lenders like this scenario?

Whose money is safer?

FIGURE 44: Would Lenders Like This Scenario?

What about the situation where the lender offers a 65% LTV loan? Do lenders like this? Of *course* they do! If the homeowner defaults, the lender could get 100% of the property for 65% of the value. The lender could also get 100% of the equity. The 35% equity, called "protective equity," is a nice cushion for the lender. This scenario allowed the lender to shift a lot more risk towards the homeowner.

What is common to all these scenarios? The risk relationship between the lender and the property owner.

LENDER RISK   BORROWER RISK

FIGURE 45: Borrower/Lender Risk Relationship

If the lender's risk goes up, the borrower's risk goes down. If the lender's risk goes down, the borrower's risk goes up. They never go in the same direction.

So risk is always being shifted away from or towards either of these two parties. The question to consider is, "Which way do *you* want the risk to be pointing?" Do you want to take more risk or less risk?

So as the lender's loan goes down (and the property owner's equity goes up), the risk is shifted away from the lender towards the property owner.

What about paying down the mortgage? What happens to the risk? Is it shifting to the lender? No, the borrower is taking on more risk and shifting it away from the lender.

Am I suggesting that you not pay down the mortgage? No, but I want you to be aware of the relationship. Also, you will need to know that there's a special way to do that, and it's not what most people think.

Lesson 1:
There is a risk relationship between the borrower and the lender.

Lesson 2:
Paying down your mortgage shifts risk to the homeowner and away from the lender, and your return on that additional payment is 0%.

Return on Equity

Consider these questions — and answers:

1. Is the equity in your home liquid?

No, you can't access that like a bank savings account.

2. How much money is it making for you?
   None.
3. How much interest do you make on your down payment or equity?
   None.
4. Will your house still appreciate the same whether you have a mortgage or not?
   Yes.
5. Will your house still appreciate the same whether you have equity or not?
   Yes.
6. Is the equity in a property safe?

Consider hurricane Katrina. During recovery from Katrina, homes were destroyed whether they had a mortgage or not. The insurance companies still have not paid some of the homeowners. And how about those homeowners who had paid off their mortgage and were debt free, but had no liquidity to buy/build another home or start a business to accrue cash for that purpose?

The headline of an article in *USA Today* — a year after hurricane Katrina — summarized this best: "Homeowners decked by Katrina still wait for insurers to pay up." People with cash in hand (i.e., those who had not used it to pay off the mortgage) were free to make choices from a wider spectrum. Do you want your money to be stuck in your property or to have cash on hand?

When you prepay your mortgage with additional payments, you shift more risk to yourself (and away from the lender), and the money you prepaid has *no return*! As a home appreciates and your home loan LTV goes down, lenders are safer and your equity becomes less safe!

Ultimately, it boils down to this. Would you prefer to have $300,000 in cash with a property worth $300,000 and a mortgage for $300,000 (zero equity), or would you prefer to have a $300,000 home that is free and clear and have no cash? Note that your net worth in either case is still $300,000.

In the first scenario, you shifted all the risk to the lender and away from you. You still have cash to live on. In the latter case, you tied up your cash into a property with 0% return. That is risky.

The Story of Two Brothers

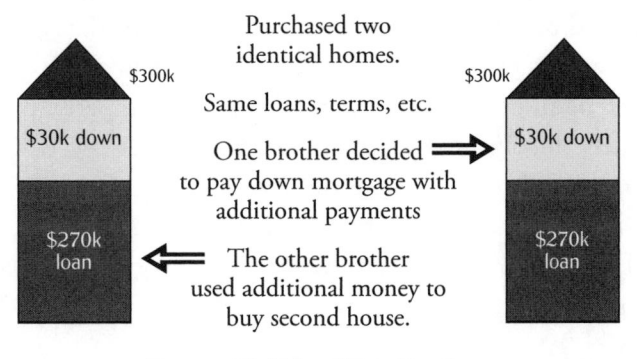

FIGURE 46: Tale of Two Brothers

Two brothers purchased two identical homes, each valued at $300,000. They got the same loan amounts. One decided to pay down his mortgage with additional payments; the other used his additional money to buy a second house.

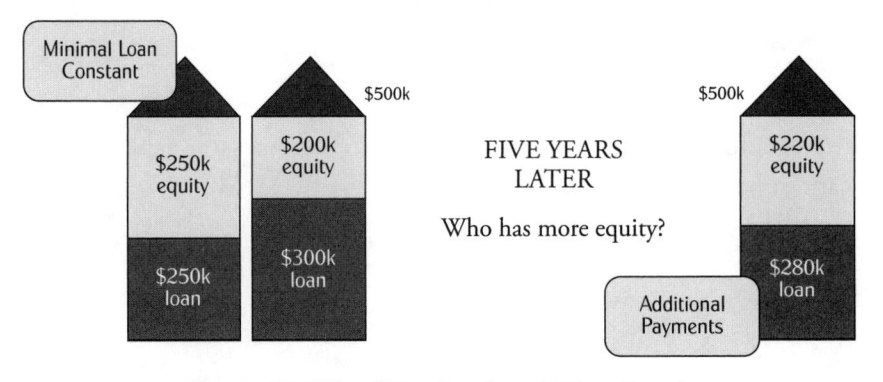

FIGURE 47: Tale of Two Brothers (5 Years Later)

Five years later both brothers' homes end up being worth $500k. The brother who paid down his mortgage now had $220k of equity in his home (see property on right-hand side in Figure 47). The other brother had $200k of equity in his own home and $250k equity in his second home, for a total of $450k equity in the two properties. Which brother did the right thing to build his equity and make his money work for him?

The second brother, with the greater equity, used the right leverage with a minimal loan constant (not necessarily the lowest interest rate). He used his additional money to buy the second property. By not paying down the mortgage, he was maintaining the same risk with the lender. The other brother (on the right) was paying down his loan with additional payments, shifting the risk away from lender and towards himself. The additional money he was using to pay down the mortgage had a return of 0%.

> ## Lesson 3:
> ### The best use of your money is to not pay down your mortgage with additional payments; rather, invest that money into acquiring more assets!

Some people say, "I want a 15-year amortized mortgage so that I can be free and clear in 15 years." That feeling is understandable. People want to be free of obligations. So consider Figure 48. Which loan would you pick?

FLEXIBLE LOAN	INFLEXIBLE LOAN
Imagine a 15-year loan that says: • Your monthy payment is $898.83. • If you lose your job or become unable to pay, you can choose to pay $583.33 until you can afford to pay the higher amount again.	Imagine a 15-year loan that says: • Your monthy payment is $898.83. • If you are unable to pay that amount, you can **lose your home** and potentially the equity you built in your home!

FIGURE 48: Which is The Better Loan?

People select the *inflexible* loan every day! The worst part is that the professionals they depend on to know this information put them in the *inflexible* loan — because *they* don't know any better!

Consider these options. Which mortgage (leverage) is best to have:

15-year loan?
30-year loan?
40-year loan?
Interest-only loan?

To best answer this question, look at the following table:

TERM AMOUNT	15-YEAR	30-YEAR	INTEREST ONLY
Loan Amount	$100,000	$100,000	$100,000
Interest Rate	7.0%	7.0%	7.0%
Monthly Payment	$ 898.83	$ 665.30	$ 583.33
Difference	$ 315.50	$ 81.97	– 0 –

As we compare these loans, we see that the biggest difference is in the monthly payment. Column one, 15-year term, can be paid off in 15 years, and in column two, the loan can be paid off in 30 years, but the loan in column three will never be paid off. Most people stop looking at this point and determine that the 15-year loan (column one) is best. However, let's dig a little deeper.

The difference between payments in the 15-year loan and the interest-only loan is $315.50. So, if you pick the interest-only loan, you're keeping $315.50 every month. If you were to use that additional money to pay down the interest-only loan, you could pay it off in 15 years!

Let me explain this differently. The monthly payment in the interest-only loan is $583.33 (as shown in the table on page 101). If you were to add $315.50 to that payment, you would be paying the *same* monthly amount as the 15-year amortized loan, and you would also pay off the interest-only loan in 15 years.

So, if you set up your loan as interest-only and pay as if it were a 15-year loan, that's how long it will take to pay it off. *But,* the good news is, if you have a few bad months, as long as you pay the interest, *you will not lose the house!* You always have the option of paying the lesser amount of $583.33. You don't *have to* pay the higher amount of $898.83!

Now, let's reconsider this figure below:

FLEXIBLE LOAN	INFLEXIBLE LOAN
Imagine a 15-year loan that says:	Imagine a 15-year loan that says:
• Your monthy payment is $898.83. • If you lose your job or become unable to pay, you can choose to pay $583.33 until you can afford to pay the higher amount again.	• Your monthy payment is $898.83. • If you are unable to pay that amount, you can **lose your home** and potentially the equity you built in your home!

FIGURE 49: Reconsider Which is The Better Loan

Read it carefully. Do you get the "ah ha"? The 15-year amortized mortgage is the inflexible loan, while the flexible one is the interest-only loan that you can pay down in 15 years if you so *choose* (a very powerful word — having the option of doing it or not doing it).

Similarly, if you took the difference between the interest-only loan and the 30-year loan — $81.97 — and add that to your interest-only payments, you could pay off that loan in 30 years!

If you add to your payment the difference between the 30-year loan and the 15-year loan, you can pay off the 30-year loan *in 15 years!*

So, in terms of risk between these loans, the interest-only loan is least risky because you always have the option to pay more.

Now, do you remember my original question: Which would you pick?

A risky loan with a low interest rate?

A less-risky loan with a slightly higher interest rate?

I hope you see where I'm leading you.

If you're a real estate professional, by now you're shouting: "George, the table on page 101 is unrealistic! The interest rates you're using for all the loans are the same. In real life, you get a lower interest rate for the 15-year amortized loan than you get with the others."

OK. Let's plug in some "real" numbers. Notice the new interest rates I'm using below.

TERM AMOUNT	15-YEAR	30-YEAR	INTEREST ONLY
Loan Amount	$100,000	$100,000	$100,000
Interest Rate	4.91%	5.17%	5.65%
Monthly Payment	$ 786.11	$ 547.26	$ 470.83
Difference	$ 315.28	$ 76.43	– 0 –
Pay Off Time	15 yrs.	16 yrs., 5 mo.	16 yrs., 5 mo.

FIGURE 50: Interest Rates for Various Mortgage Periods

Notice the lower interest rate for the 15-year than the 30-year and the interest-only loans. The banks are using this as "bait" to make you take the higher-risk loan (the 15-year loan) instead of the 30-year loan. Consumers have been conditioned to pick the lower interest rate and 15-year loan so they can be debt-free sooner.

Notice the difference between the 15-year payment ($786.11) and the interest-only payment ($470.83). With a 15-year loan you're betting that nothing bad is going to happen over the next 15 years; whereas, with the interest-only loan, you can choose to pay the higher payment, or not.

In other words, by getting a 15-year amortized loan, you're paying the higher amount of $786.11 for 15 straight years. *That's* what I call risky! You're taking a much higher payment and paying down the mortgage fast. However, at the same time, you're shifting the risk away from the lender to yourself, and if you have a few bad months anytime in the 15 years, you can lose your property. So, you're taking a lot more risk for 15 straight years to get a return of 0% on that additional money and putting your wealth at risk.

If you apply the difference from the 15-year rate, it will take slightly longer to pay off the loan — actually 16 years and 5 months. If you apply the difference from the 30-year rate, you can also pay off the loan in 16 years and 5 months. *And* you don't have the flexibility to pay less with either of those loans. So the 15-year loan is the riskiest because of its inflexibility.

This, again, illustrates the difference between risky and managing risk. Savvy wealth builders manage risk, while those who don't know better take the risky 15-year mortgage.

Now, let's go back to the question I asked about a flexible and an inflexible 15-year loan. You should have selected the interest-only loan with choices. This is very flexible, and flexibility is what you want.

So the least risky loan is the interest-only, followed by the 40-year loan, the 30-year loan, and the 15-year loan. Go for the longest time factor because that gives you the opportunity to design your own loan based on what you want to pay.

The next question is, "Which loan is best for cash flow?" Isn't it the loan with the lowest interest rate?

Lesson 4:
A 15-year amortized loan is
built into a 30-year amortized loan.
A 30-year amortized loan is built into a
40-year amortized loan. All of those in turn
are built into an interest-only loan!

The best loan for cash flow is the one with the best loan constant, as I've covered in previous chapters. To maximize your cash flow, you want to minimize your loan constant. By doing this you minimize the cash *outflow* from your pocket. Because there is principal and interest involved in getting a loan, you can't simply judge by the interest rate. You must choose the loan with the lowest loan constant.

Take another look at the example I covered before:

LOAN 1	LOAN 2	LOAN 3	LOAN 4
5.50%	6.8%	8.2%	7.8%
5-year fixed amortized	30-year fixed amortized	10-year fixed interest-only	15-year fixed amortized

Which loan has the lowest loan constant?
FIGURE 51: VARIOUS LOANS AND LOAN CONSTANTS

Which loan has the lowest loan constant? (Use the downloaded calculator to calculate it). If you're buying a rental property, which of these loans would you want to get? Actually, the best loan for this investment is loan no. 2 because the loan constant is low. (Answers to the loan constant table above are in a previous table shown in Figure 15 on page 47.)

> ## Lesson 5:
> In most cases, the best mortgage for investors is a loan with the lowest loan constant.
>
> ## Lesson 6:
> To pick the right loan, you need to identify the lowest cost of money for you over the years.

Should I Pay Points on the Loan?

Sometimes when you're trying to obtain a mortgage (or leverage) to buy an asset, you're faced with either paying points and having a lower interest rate or paying no points with a higher interest rate. These are called "buy-down points."

Which option works best for you? Refer to the Cost of Money Calculator found in the Resources section. Simply calculate how it affects your loan over time. First, determine how long you'll be keeping the property.

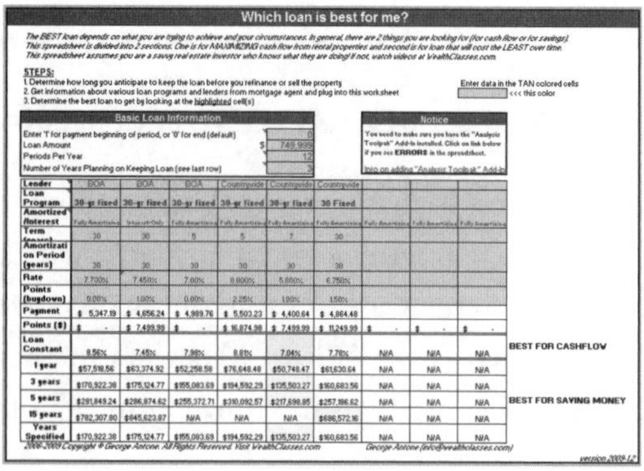

FIGURE 52: Snapshot of the Cost of Money Calculator

Ask your mortgage professional for various loan programs. Plug the numbers into the calculator and determine — according to your needs and what you've learned here — which loan package is the best for any deal.

Sometimes it makes sense to pay the buy-down points because, in the long run, it ends up costing you less — much less. The key is to ask yourself this: What is my exit strategy, my plan for the property? Do I want to sell it in 5 years? Do I want to hold on to it for 20 years as a rental property? Is this for cash flow? Do I want the least costly loan? The answers to all these questions will help you decide whether or not to purchase buy-down points.

Remember, as a savvy wealth builder, you should use leverage to build wealth, and you need to become efficient in using leverage.

Lesson 7:
Buy-down points might benefit you.
Analyze the numbers and find out.

Better Way to Pay Off Your Mortgage

Earlier, I mentioned that paying down your mortgage is shifting risk away from the lender and towards yourself. Am I suggesting that you *not* pay down a mortgage? No.

But there is a better way to do it than most people realize. Most people apply additional monthly payments to their mortgage to pay it down. Others do a bimonthly program to pay it down. These do work, but they're not the most efficient way. In fact, by doing that, you're taking more risk than you need to, as I explained in Lessons 1 and 2 earlier in this chapter.

So what's the best way?

Most people live paycheck to paycheck. That means their money sits in the bank from days to weeks until it's used to pay bills. What if you could pay off your mortgage from the *flow of money* in your life?

BETTER DEAL?

You have $1,000. You have two buckets.

Where would you put the $1,000? Do you still have access to the money if it goes into LOC?

FIGURE 53: Two Buckets (Scenario I)

Let's say that you have $1,000 and two buckets (refer to the figure above): one bucket pays 1%, and the other bucket saves 6%. Bucket 1 is a checking account where you're earning 1% interest (if you're lucky) and paying taxes on the interest you earned. The second bucket is a line of credit with $2,000 debt in there. If you place the $1,000 there, you're saving 6% interest on the $1,000 that you would have had to pay. So bucket 1 is earning 1%, while bucket 2 is saving you 6%.

Where would you put the $1,000? Bucket 1 or 2?

Consider bucket 2. If you placed the $1,000 there, is it liquid? Do you still have access to the money if it goes into the line of credit? Of course. So it's better to place the $1,000 into bucket 2, because while it's sitting there for the few weeks before you pay your bills, you've saved

BETTER DEAL?

You have $1,000. You have two buckets.

Where would you put the $1,000? Do you still have access to the money if it goes into loan?

FIGURE 54: Two Buckets (Scenario II)

108

6% for those few weeks. You didn't have to pay taxes on the savings. Also, saving 6% is equivalent to earning 6% tax-free.

Let's add another wrinkle. You have $1,000 and two buckets. The first bucket is the checking account paying 1% interest, and the second bucket is a $10k car loan (debt). Where would you put the $1,000?

In this case (Figure 54), the checking account is the better bet, because what you pay down on the car loan may save you some percentage of interest, but then the money isn't available to you for use. You can't pay the bills from it. That's called a closed loan. Once you pay it, you don't have access to it. With a line of credit, you have access.

BETTER DEAL?

You have $1,000. You have 1 of 3 places to put it.

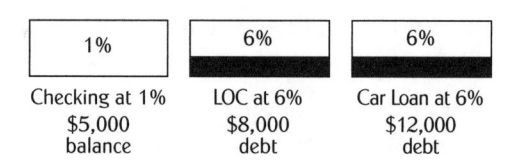

Checking at 1%	LOC at 6%	Car Loan at 6%
$5,000	$8,000	$12,000
balance	debt	debt

Where would you put the $1,000?

FIGURE 55: Three Buckets (Scenario III)

The third scenario is that you have $1,000 and three buckets (Figure 55). The first bucket is the checking account with a $5,000 balance and with interest accruing at 1%. The second bucket is the line of credit at 6% that is up to $8,000 debt. The third bucket is a $12,000 car loan at 6% interest. Where would you put your $1,000?

Because the money is still liquid, parking it in the line of credit is the right answer. Here it maintains its liquidity, and it saves you 6% interest for the period during which it is parked.

Now assume that you have that same old $1,000 and the same buckets (Figure 56). Your checking account pays 1% interest, and you pay taxes on the earnings. The 6% line of credit has zero debt. And the third bucket is a $12,000 car loan at 6% interest. Where would you put your $1,000?

Think about it before moving on.

BETTER DEAL?

You have $1,000. You have 1 of 3 places to put it.

1%	6%	6%
Checking at 1% $5,000 balance	LOC at 6% $0 debt	Car Loan at 6% $12,000 debt

Where would you put the $1,000?

FIGURE 56: Three Buckets (Scenario IV)

Here's the answer: Use the open line of credit to pay down the car loan. This made you shift debt from a closed loan to the line of credit. So now the car loan has been paid down, and the line of credit has debt.

Now, park the $1,000 in the line of credit until you use it to pay bills. For the time it's in that account, you'll be "earning" 6% — tax-free.

Therefore, instead of parking money in a checking account until you pay your bills, by parking your money in a line of credit, you can lower the *effective* interest rate on a temporary basis. That would result in paying off your mortgage in one-half to one-third the time without making additional mortgage payments every month. This is using the *flow of money* to pay off your mortgages and leverage *fast*.

There's a lot more information about this in my Debt Management System program (refer to the Resources section).

> ## Lesson 8:
> ## To pay off your mortgage fast,
> ## use the Debt Management System.

Leverage Equity into Wealth

Let's look at two properties and deals (below). Both are valued at $300,000. The property on the left has a loan for $300,000 with zero equity in the property. You have $100,000 in cash, though. The second property (on the right) has $100,000 cash put into it as a down payment (therefore, equity) and a $200,000 loan. Which one should you pick?

WHICH SCENARIO WOULD YOU PICK?

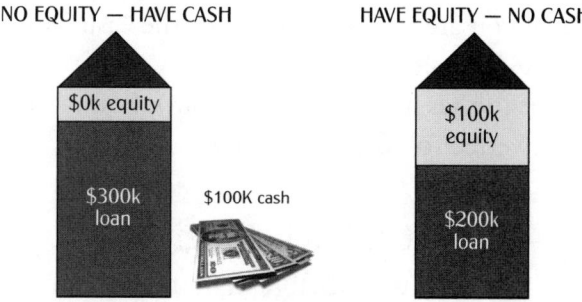

FIGURE 57: Which of the Two Scenarios is Better for Investor?

I hope you picked the left-hand one. By now, you should understand why. Most people pick the scenario with one-third in for the equity and a $200k mortgage. But this is not the better of the two because the buyer is taking on risk and doesn't have the cash to use if and when he needs it.

I hope you know the "Golden Rule."

The Golden Rule:
Those who have the gold make the rules.

Here are some related "truths":

- Americans don't save money.
- We're used to spending everything.
- As a result, someone else must provide the capital necessary to sustain our way of life. This strategy carries with it a very high cost, because those with the capital make the rules, and we all suffer the consequences! Look around you. Who has the money? They are the ones making the rules we have to live by.
- When someone has a large amount of cash on hand, all sorts of good opportunities appear, and very favorable purchase prices can be negotiated. When you are the one who holds the cash, you are the one who can make the rules.
- Equity can be lost (as many are finding out). Equity means nothing until it is converted to cash or cash flow.

> ## Capital is King!
> ## It's about Control!
> ## Don't forget "The Golden Rule."
> ## When you have a chance to hold cash
> ## versus equity, cash is always King!

So How Do You Leverage Equity into Wealth?

Before I even begin on this point, you need to recognize and accept that equity earns 0%; therefore, it does nothing for anyone. However, equity is a perfect vehicle to use for leverage — positive leverage.

Here's what you need to know. You can turn equity into a mortgage (the mortgage could be a second loan) or HELOC (Home Equity Line of Credit). You need to know how to pick the right vehicle for the right investment. Let's look at these vehicles and when to use them.

HELOC is best used for:

- Short-time deals (less than a year).
- Arbitrage (short-term; e.g., lending).
- Turning money fast (the "velocity of money") for buying a property at under market value, refinancing, and then paying back the HELOC.
- Buying undervalued assets for quick turns when you're not going to hold onto it. Do not use a HELOC for a down payment, because HELOCs have an adjustable interest rate, and the investment has a fixed capitalization rate, as explained in previous chapters. HELOCs translate to variable loan constants. We need to manage risk — also explained in previous chapters.

Mortgage is best used:

- To fix the cost of money and loan constant
- For down payment on other positive-leveraged assets
- For appreciating assets
- For long-term arbitrage
- For "buy and hold" strategy

Lesson 9:
One of the fastest ways to a high net worth is through the use of the right leverage and by using the "power of finance" to pay it off!

Lesson 10:
Match the investment to the type of vehicle you will use to extract your money from the equity (HELOC or mortgage).

The Mortgage Team

- You need to have a good mortgage broker on your team.
- The broker needs to understand your goals.
- The broker needs to understand everything in this book.
- Brokers will resist, but you need to share your knowledge by exposing them to this book.
- Your broker probably will dismiss this information to justify their position! It usually takes me three times longer to get through to brokers because of their resistance to listening! And they need to know this stuff. I estimate that 99% of investors and mortgage brokers have not heard of a loan constant.

> One simple decision affects your
> economic future. Choose the right broker.

"How was that?" I smiled, hoping I had passed the test. I had just spent a lot of time recapping everything he had taught me.

"Wow! Great job. You got it. I'm impressed. So you do have some brain cells up there."

We laughed.

CHAPTER SUMMARY

- Lesson 1: Understand there is risk relationship between the borrower and the lender.
- Lesson 2: Paying down your mortgage shifts more risk to the homeowner and away from the lender, and your return on that additional payment is 0%.
- Lesson 3: The best use of your money is to not pay down your mortgage with additional payments; rather, invest that money into acquiring more assets!
- Lesson 4: Recognize that a 15-year amortized loan is built into a 30-year amortized loan, which is built into an interest-only loan!
- Lesson 5: In most cases, the best mortgage for investors (for cash flow) is a loan with the lowest loan constant.
- Lesson 6: When you pick the right loan, you need to identify the lowest cost of money for you over the years.
- Lesson 7: Buy-down points might benefit you. Analyze the numbers and find out.
- Lesson 8: To pay off your mortgage fast, use the Debt Management System.
- Lesson 9: One of the fastest ways to a high net worth is to select the right leverage and use "the power of finance" to pay it off!
- Lesson 10: Match the investment to the type of vehicle you will use to extract your money from the equity (HELOC or mortgage).
- Pick a mortgage team that understands the concepts in this book.
- The type of loan you want has the lowest:
    1. Loan constant
    2. Risk
    3. Interest rate

CHAPTER ELEVEN

I Finally *Got* Leverage

"What do you think is the fastest way to make $1,000,000?"
I knew the answer to that, but I went for the joke instead.
"Marry a rich woman?" I said with a straight face. "Rob a bank?
Borrow enough money to make it?"
"Bingo! The fastest way to make $1,000,000 is to use leverage to
buy assets worth 10 to 20 times the money you want to have," he
laughed. "Problem is, most people are uncomfortable getting into that
much debt. But that's the way I became wealthy. And you can, too.
Anybody can."

THAT DAY MY LIFE CHANGED. COMBINING WHAT I HAD LEARNED FROM Robert Kiyosaki's books and my mentor's advice, the world of the wealthy became possible. I finally "got it"! And I can explain what "it" is using these statements:

- The fastest way to get out of the rat race is to use leverage — the right kind of leverage.
- Wealth comes from creating safe spreads that generate nice cash flow monthly.

- Leverage can make you wealthy if you know how to use it, measure it, and manage it. Leverage can be positive, neutral, and negative. The wealthy use positive leverage to become wealthy.
- The wealthy understand how to manage risk and never do risky things. They also know when to use debt financing and when to use equity financing. They understand risk and how to share it and shift it.

Ignorant Statements From the Media

Recently, I saw an article on *Yahoo!* offering reasons not to buy real estate but to rent instead. When I read this article I was blown away at how ignorant the writer was. I did further research and found many articles on this subject. Unfortunately, these articles are being read by the masses, and these misinformed pieces help shape people's beliefs. That's why the poor and middle class think differently than the rich — they read and believe articles written by people who are not qualified to be writing about money.

Let's review some common statements by uninformed (ignorant) writers that offered, on various websites, reasons for not buying real estate. My comments and opinions on each "reason" follow.

"Real estate has appreciated only 1% over inflation since 1969."

Let's assume 5% appreciation and that inflation is 4%. So the (ignorant) statement above is true if an investor is buying all cash with no leverage. But if you use positive leverage (which savvy investors do), your *total* return (including all profit centers mentioned before) can be as little as 20% or as much as 80%! So, adjusted to inflation, we're talking about a 16% to 76% return. Where else can you find this kind of return for investment?

"Home appreciation figures don't take into account all the money people pour into their houses in the form of repairs and upgrades."

In our model we already have built in the required funding for repairs and maintenance. Remember TIMMUR? Taxes, insurance, management, maintenance, utilities, and repair. So with positive leverage, we have not only cash flow after all expenses and mortgage, we also keep all the appreciation!

"Some of the people who tell me I'm throwing money away on rent are people with interest-only mortgages. They're not building equity."

Interest-only mortgages are good because they have the lowest loan constants. The lowest loan constants result in the biggest spread, which means the best cash flow. What people need to realize is that loans with low loan constants are the least risky loans. The loans with the highest loan constants are the highest risk to the homeowner. With interest-only loans, you minimize risk and maximize cash flow and appreciation. You're still building appreciation while minimizing risk!

"I think the 15-year fixed is the only mortgage to choose. If you have to get a 30-year mortgage to make your payments, you're trying to buy more house than you can afford — look elsewhere. Thirty-year mortgages are financially deadly."

What an ignorant thing to say! I wish I had more space to explain this. Suffice it to say that the 30-year mortgage loan constant is better than a 15-year. Most people pick the 15-year fixed mortgage because that's what they've been told. The worst and most risky loan to get is the 15-year mortgage; better is the 30-year mortgage; and the best of this kind is the 40-year mortgage. Interest-only beats them all! For homeowners, 15-year loans are the riskiest loans, because they have the highest loan constants, as I explained in Chapter 10.

Don't be ignorant! Take the time to educate yourself about how to use your money wisely to get the best return. By reading this book you're on the right track. I've included more resources for further education in the Resources section. Refer to these resources for more-detailed information about some points I've barely touched on. Do that, and you *won't* be one of those who make ignorant statements such as the ones above.

To review the statement made in my introduction: The fastest way to massive wealth is with leverage, the right kind of leverage! I hope this statement makes complete sense to you now.

"So, George, are you going to go out and implement these strategies?"

"Of course" I said confidently. "Consider it done."

"You realize that most people talk, but very few people take action and make a decision to move forward. I just want to make sure you're absolutely committed to doing this."

"Absolutely," I confirmed.

CHAPTER SUMMARY

- Understand leverage and use it. You'll be on your way to joining the wealthy.
- Ignore ignorant statements in the media. Becoming wealthy is more possible than ever. It's been proven throughout history. It boils down to understanding The Wealthy Code.

CHAPTER TWELVE

Applying Wealth Strategies

"My mind is more than fried," I said as I rested my head in my hands. "This was a serious overload. But I get it; it's a piece of art! Give me some real-life examples on how to use leverage."

"Well, George, I'll share with you a few examples of leverage, but I haven't shared the really big 'ah-ha' yet. I'll reveal that right after the examples so you can appreciate how powerful it is."

THUS FAR I'VE FOCUSED ON THE MIDDLE COLUMN THAT MY MENTOR introduced me to, the Cash Flow column. Again, I'm using the definition of wealth by Robert Kiyosaki: having enough monthly passive cash flow to cover your monthly expenses.

Cash flow comes from arbitrage (the spread between inflow of cash and outflow of cash). There are three kinds of arbitrage:

- Pure (or true)
- Near
- Speculative

The first of these three is the pure, "riskless," version (according to the definition of "arbitrage" at *investopedia.com*). The second kind, or "near arbitrage," is almost risk-free, but the risk is manageable. The third kind is "speculative arbitrage," or more-risky arbitrage. I won't be talking about that in this book.

The first one, pure arbitrage, is hard to find in real life. The best one to focus on is the "near" arbitrage, because it can be found out there and the risk can be managed.

The strategies I'll offer in this chapter are for near arbitrage. I'll provide examples that apply what we've learned so far, and I'll cover income properties (real estate) and other non-real-estate-related investments.

Strategy One:
Income Properties (Real Estate)

For income properties I'll use apartment buildings as an example. By definition, apartment buildings are 5 or more units; I'll be talking about 15-unit properties or more to mediate the risk.

Let's go back to an example from an earlier chapter. You walk into a retail store and see two ATMs for sale.

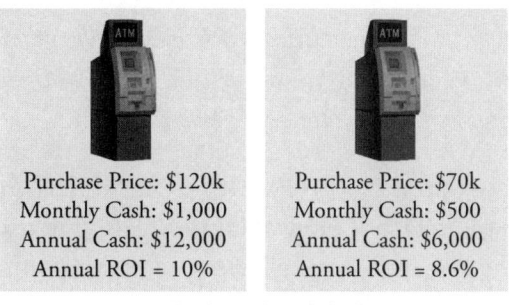

Purchase Price: $120k	Purchase Price: $70k
Monthly Cash: $1,000	Monthly Cash: $500
Annual Cash: $12,000	Annual Cash: $6,000
Annual ROI = 10%	Annual ROI = 8.6%

Which is a better deal?

FIGURE 58: Example of Two Special ATM Machines (I)

As before, they look identical, but the one on the left has a price tag of $120,000; the one on the right is $70,000. (Remember the price of each machine.) These are special ATM machines in that when you stand in front of each of them on the first of each month, they allow a certain amount of money to come out. The one on the left releases $1,000 per month, and the one on the right releases $500 per month.

So, do you remember which one is the better deal?

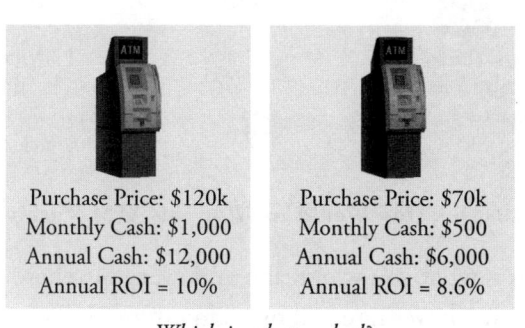

Purchase Price: $120k	Purchase Price: $70k
Monthly Cash: $1,000	Monthly Cash: $500
Annual Cash: $12,000	Annual Cash: $6,000
Annual ROI = 10%	Annual ROI = 8.6%

Which is a better deal?

FIGURE 59: Example of Two Special ATM Machines (II)

Let me give you the same hint I gave you back in that earlier chapter — the annual cash flow of the ATM on the left is $12,000. That's the monthly cash flow multiplied by 12. The ATM on the right has an annual cash flow of $6,000.

As you may recall, the ATM on the left is the better deal. You figure that out by dividing the annual cash flow by the price you paid to get the return. That makes the cash-on-cash return of the ATM on the left 10%; the one on the right is 8.6%.

However, it so happens that you don't have the money to pay cash for the machine you have chosen — the ATM on the left. Let's assume your Uncle John has $120,000 in the bank getting a 3% interest rate. You convince him to lend you that $120,000, secured by the ATM machine, at 7%. So now the ATM pays you 10%, and you pay Uncle John 7%. The machine releases $1,000 on the first of the month, and you pay Uncle John $700, giving you a 3% spread and passive income of $300 each and every month.

In terms of income properties, the income property itself is the ATM machine; Uncle John represents the institutional lenders.

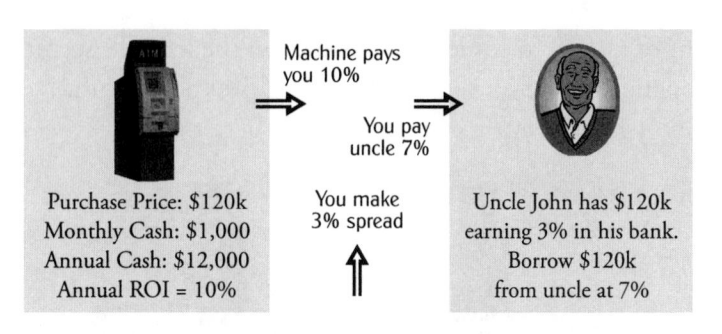

Purchase Price: $120k
Monthly Cash: $1,000
Annual Cash: $12,000
Annual ROI = 10%

Machine pays
you 10%

You pay
uncle 7%

You make
3% spread

Uncle John has $120k
earning 3% in his bank.
Borrow $120k
from uncle at 7%

FIGURE 60: How Would You *Buy* This ATM Machine?

In essence, this is what you want each and every purchase to do for you. Borrow money at a lower rate and buy something that gives you a higher return.

For example, buy a building for $2 million using leverage where the loan constant is lower than the cap rate or when the building is paying you more than what you are paying the lender. Perhaps the building pays you 9% annually, you pay the bank 7%, and you make a 2% spread. You keep the spread (the arbitrage). That gives you the cash flow.

Here's another example. To get an apartment building you decide to borrow 75% from the bank (at the rate of 7.5%) with a 10% loan from the seller at 7% (also known as "seller financing"), and the property has a 9% cap rate. You created positive leverage off both the lender's and the seller's money.

Let's compare the difference between apartments and single-family residences (SFR). See Figure 61.

Single-family residences, as rentals, in general, are not good cash-flow-making vehicles. Notice, I stated that carefully, because there are various strategies that can make SFRs great for cash flow. That is not covered in this book.

Let's continue with income properties. I touched on Net Operating Income (NOI) earlier. In its basic form, NOI is nothing more than the difference between the income and the expenses.

So let's consider this building (Figure 62).

APARTMENTS	SINGLE-FAMILY RESIDENCES
Lenders qualify property first	Lenders qualify borrower first
Valued by income	Valued by comps
Lender *wants* you to make money	Lender does not care if you make money
Cash flow is better	Appreciates faster *(in appreciating markets)*
2 to 3 deals from "wealthy"	*Many* deals away from "wealthy" (if at all)
Good vehicle for becoming "wealthy"	Good vehicle to build equity and move into apartments

FIGURE 61: Comparison between Apartments and SFRs

NOI = Net Operating Income
NOI = Income – Expenses
Cap Rate = NOI/Building price

DESCRIPTION	AMOUNT
Building Price...$550,000	
Income $100,000	
Expenses ....– $ 45,000	
Net Operating Income (NOI) ....$ 55,000	
Debt Service (Mortgage)..– $ 44,000	
Cash Flow...$ 11,000	

FIGURE 62: Example of Building Numbers

Again, NOI is the difference between income and expenses. Expenses do not include mortgage payments (known as "debt service"). It includes TIMMUR (covered in Chapter 4).

So the cap rate is calculated as:

Cap Rate = NOI/Price = $55k/$550k = 10%

Apartments are a great way to become wealthy. In an interview published in the Summer 2006 issue of *Creative Real Estate Lifestyles*, page 46, Robert Kiyosaki said that it was cash flow from his apartment buildings that allowed him to retire and write the book, *Rich Dad Poor Dad*.

In the bestselling book, *Trump: The Art of the Deal*, Donald Trump describes how his father built his wealth with apartment buildings. Many wealthy people have used this same vehicle to build wealth.

The object of this section is to introduce you to the basics of this vehicle to build wealth. It's not the real estate — brick and mortar — that excites wealth builders; it's the ability to get financing (leverage) against it while it generates income (just like the ATM machine) that makes it interesting. Income properties allow us to generate positive leverage to help generate cash flow. It's nothing more than a financing game.

Wealth is nothing more than a financing game!

It's not about the real estate. It's about the ability to use the real estate as collateral to generate financing — and a spread.

Strategy Two: Private Lending

In this section I will describe how to use private lending to generate cash flow, specifically, how to *be* a private lender. Let's start by considering what a bank does.

We've been programmed to save money in the bank. When we do that, we're actually lending our money to the bank for practically nothing.

For the sake of this example, let's say we get paid 2% from our savings account. So the banks borrow our money for 2% and then they lend it back to us as a mortgage for 6% or more. They created the spread (4%) we have been talking about all along!

As private lenders, we can do the same thing. We can borrow money at a lower rate and lend it out securely as a mortgage at a higher rate.

How would you like to build wealth:

- Without buying properties?
- Without applying for a mortgage?
- Without managing tenants?
- Without using your own money?
- Without using your credit?

This is the power of private lending. Private lending has existed for decades for a good reason. It's safe and lucrative! The concept of private lending is extremely powerful! Let me share with you some private lending "magic" that will work for you.

In this scenario, I'm not using leverage — simply arbitrage. Let's say you borrow $100,000 at 8% from an OPM source. You lend this out securely (backed by real estate) at 15%. By the end of the year you would receive $15,000 in interest alone. You need to pay $8,000 to the source of your $100,000 loan, so you are left with $7,000 out of every $100,000 of OPM. This is good, but it's not so exciting.

Let's make it more exciting by adding 3:1 ratio leverage to the formula. The first thing you do is borrow the same $100,000 (OPM) at 8%. You leverage to $300,000 at 8% (3:1 ratio) and lend all $400,000 at 15% securely. You receive $60,000 by the end of the year from the $400,000 lent out. Now you have to pay the two sources — the leverage ($24,000) and the private source ($8,000) — for a total of $32,000. This means your net income would be $28,000 every year for every $100,000 of OPM. This feels much more exciting.

And to extend that example, if you were to raise $400,000 of OPM (instead of the $100,000 of OPM in the previous paragraph), that would correspond to a net income of $112,000 for the year. That's four times the $28,000 calculated in the previous paragraph because you raised four times the $100,000 of OPM. All using positive leverage.

Let's make this even a little more exciting. Let's look at 4:1 ratio leverage. It's the same thing, but now we're playing with bigger numbers. We'll have you borrow $100,000 OPM at 8% and leverage it up to $400,000 at 8%. Take the $500,000 and lend it at 15% securely. You'll receive $75,000 in interest and pay out $40,000, netting $35,000 for every $100,000 of OPM!

Wait. It gets better!

So far, I've been talking about debt financing. As you may recall, debt financing is where you're paying someone an interest rate. This is just borrowing money at a certain interest. But there's something called "equity financing," too. Equity financing is when you get a percentage of the profit. You lend someone money, and they pay back your money with a percentage of the profit.

For example, I lend you money for 50% of the profit. There is no interest component. However, you can combine debt financing and equity financing. So I can lend money at a certain interest rate, and I'll also take a portion of the profit. This is a combination loan.

Since we're talking about combining debt and equity financing, let's make this clearer and really exciting, by using the same example from above.

We'll have you borrow $100,000 at 8%, leverage it up 4:1, for $400,000, and then lend this out at 15% for a part of the profit (equity financing). So you'll get back $75,000 in interest and $100,000 in profit

— in addition to the interest. When you pay back your source of money, you're paying back at only 8%, so you pay out $40,000, leaving you with $135,000 net income every year for every $100,000 of OPM!

Now we can get really excited because this is fabulous!

This is certainly more complicated and more advanced, but the key here is that private lending is nothing more than a financing game as well. Notice that we do all this with nothing more than leverage, the right kind of leverage.

Is it starting to sound familiar? By using the same strategies that banks have used for hundreds of years, we can generate positive leverage that helps generate cash flow! Lending is about lending and has nothing to do with real estate, except to use other people's real estate as collateral. Everything I've been writing about in this book, whether in real estate or private lending, involves generating wealth using spreads.

Let's move on to the next wealth vehicle.

Strategy Three: Insurance Arbitrage

How would you like to create a steady annual six-figure, passive, tax-free income for the rest of your life (well, until you're 120 years old at least — after that you're on your own) starting in only 10 to 15 years by simply using the power of positive leverage?

Without real estate or private lending, you can create this type of income stream. This strategy is for those who can qualify: high-net-worth individuals and business owners. The asset class I'm talking about begins by leveraging your economic value. This value builds upon your income and asset base. The qualities of this funding vehicle are amazing, and although it has been used by the wealthy and banks for decades, it still remains misunderstood, if not relatively unknown.

Using a properly constructed and managed "insurance arbitrage" strategy, you can create for yourself a passive six-figure tax-free income for the rest of your life. If you were to set up this strategy today and knew you would make $25,000 per month to age 120 starting 10 to

15 years from now, wouldn't you jump at it? Imagine having money you could count on at a time in your life when you need it most!

Let's look at the basic idea. Understand that, again, I'm still just talking about leverage. Let's say that a bank will lend you funds at 5% and your asset will pay, on average, 8%, for a 3% spread. But what will you use for collateral? The bank will use your asset (insurance policy), which you buy as collateral in many cases, to secure the financing. Depending on how this transaction is structured and future performance, additional collateral may be needed for a period of time as well.

What if the collateral is a life insurance policy paying 8% annually? We're still talking about a 3% spread. We've found another vehicle that has allowed us to build an arbitrage opportunity for ourselves.

This type of funding vehicle, however, has some powerful additional features, including guarantees, tax treatment, and method in which the cash grows. There is no other financial vehicle like it.

Many banks love to use life insurance policies as collateral; some actually prefer them. Why do I care what the asset is as long as the bank will lend me the money using this asset as security?

It would be nice to have a fixed "cost of funds," but that's not reality in this case. Loans for apartment buildings may be fixed, but often financing against a life insurance policy involves a variable cost of funds. So let's look at the risks of having a variable cost of funds.

First of all, why worry about the financing? As I explained earlier, we need to manage the risks so that we can mitigate (i.e., lower) them. For instance, if the cost of funds starts out lower than the performance from the asset (with insurance policies, we do not use cap rates — we refer to performance) but increases and becomes higher than the performance of the asset, we have negative leverage. Suddenly, the deficit payment is coming out of our own pockets! That's a game we don't want to play.

So we need to mitigate negative leverage; we want to understand the risk, and manage it. For instance, we want to avoid highly volatile leverage, as described before. We need to look for more-stable, less-volatile

As a wealth builder, you will need
to answer these questions:
- Where can I get financing?
- What collateral do they want?
- Is this collateral (or asset) going to
  pay more than the bank financing?
- Can I manage the risk associated
  with this spread?
That's what building wealth is all about!
It's just a financing game.

leverage. If we can find a fixed-rate cost of funds, that's ideal, but in many cases we can't.

There are things we can do to minimize risk on the financing side by minimizing volatility. Here are a couple of things to consider:

- Find financing that uses a more-stable index, such as LIBOR (London Interbank Offered Rate), see page 77.
- Find financing that will change the cost of funds only once per year or longer.

For example, if the cost of funds is LIBOR + 2% and LIBOR is 3%, then the cost of funds is 5%.

So what is the performance of the asset that we're using as collateral in this transaction? We've spoken of the bank financing side so far. Now let's look at the collateral side: the life insurance policy and its performance (how it pays).

A 3% or 4% spread is great, but the asset also has a variable performance. Again, it would be nice to have a fixed return/performance that is higher than cost of funds, but that's not reality. What do we want to have in a variable performance from the policy? We need a consistent return over an extended period of time.

For example, we can't just go on "projected return." We need to look at an extended period over the past 20 years (or as long as it has existed). That will provide a basis for a decision.

We need to look for an asset that is stable with low volatility. With a stable cost of funds, a stable performance from an asset, and a wide enough spread, we will be assured of a nice, consistent spread. That way we can manage the risk and minimize the downside of this kind of funding vehicle for building long-term wealth.

An equity-index-based policy has performed at 9.51% over the past 23 years. This will give us a spread of 4% or 5% if LIBOR + 2 (4%) is the cost of funds. These specially designed insurance policies are also very powerful because the downside index credit is capped at 0% with a guaranteed minimum of 2%.

For instance, if the S&P 500 goes down so that the index goes negative relative to the previous year's performance, you will get a 0% index credit rather than actually losing principal plus your previous year's earnings. The insurance company covers this. This is one major reason why the bank prefers this kind of collateral.

Another reason this type of contract is preferred is that the indexes used to measure the growth in the contract reset each year on the policy's anniversary. In 2008, when the index markets dropped some 40%, contract holders lost nothing. With the big rebound going into 2009, some contract holders received better than 50% growth in their policy's cash account in one year.

Let's make this more interesting. What if the cost of funds is accruing? "Huh? What does that mean?" you ask. It means that you don't pay it every month. This allows the life insurance policy to grow and compound in a tax-free environment.

"And what does *that* mean?" The insurance policy is growing very quickly in a tax-free environment, and the bank financing does not get paid back until such time as there is plenty of cash in the policy to pay the loan. If the policy pays 9% and the cost of funds is still LIBOR + 2%, you have a nice spread, building the value of the asset without paying for it until the policy matures and the loan comes due. The loan is paid by netting out of the insurance cash account on a tax-free basis. This leaves an enormous sum still inside your policy's cash account to compound tax-free and to be available for a passive tax-free income on into the future.

The Three-Step Process to a Six-Figure Income

1. The bank finances your life insurance policy with little money out of your pocket. They will need some additional collateral in the first several years.

2. The policy pays the bank at the end of the 10 years or according to how and when the initial set-up structure was designed to pay back from the accrued interest and principal — all without you making monthly payments.

3. You receive annual six-figure payments for the rest of your life, until the ripe old age of 120 years.

When I plugged in the numbers and ran this scenario for a 40-year-old man, after 10 years his income ran about $400,000 per year for the rest of his life!

Here's another dramatic example of this type of funding vehicle. A 27-year-old professional ball player, who could afford to self-fund with $200,000 for 5 years, is projected to consistently receive some $155,000 per year, tax-free, starting at age 40 until age 120, at which point he would have more than $166,000,000 in cash left over! Yes, it's true. Read that number again: $166 million after receiving $155,000 per year, tax-free, for 80 years!

The objective of this section has been to illustrate that it's possible to generate wealth with vehicles other than real estate. Remember, it's a *financing game* using leverage to create pure arbitrage or near arbitrage to generate cash flow.

Strategy Four: Low-Tech Businesses

A "low-tech" business is any enterprise that uses low- to middle-skilled workers — such as a fast-food restaurant, a dry-cleaner, or a retail store at a mall. These businesses are run with a system; it's not necessary to physically be there all the time to run the business.

When a low-tech business is valued, it traditionally has low multipliers. The effect of this is that the equivalent to the cap rate (I've described this for apartment buildings) for low-tech businesses is high, as much as 20% to 30%. Let's use an average of 25%. Why is that important? Traditional financing for small businesses, for example from the Small Business Association (SBA), has a high loan constant as well.

Someone just getting into this might look at the interest rate of a business loan at 5%, for example, and say, "Wow, that's really cheap!" But we're talking about not focusing on the interest rate but the loan constant. The equivalent loan constant of SBA financing could be more than 20%! So, what does that mean? You've bought a business with a cap rate of 25%, and the loan constant is 20%, giving a spread of 5%. That would be all right except for the fact that these businesses are highly volatile.

With low-tech businesses, we need a much better spread than 5%. My mentor taught me to borrow against real estate with a loan constant of 6%. We need to buy a low-tech business with a 25% cap rate using leverage against real estate to obtain a much lower loan constant and with a nice spread that can protect against fluctuation (volatility).

So, how do we borrow against real estate? This is what one of my mentors does. He finds people who own property — especially undeveloped land — free and clear, because it's not generating any cash flow, and puts the land into a trust or an LLC (Limited Liability Corporation). He then takes that to the bank as collateral for a loan at a 6% (for example) interest rate, and then buys the business for a cap rate of 25%. That's a spread of 19%. Once again, we're talking about nothing more than spreads, but this spread is really higher than others due to the volatility of businesses in general.

Conclusion

There are many more strategies to create wealth. This has been just a sampling. You might say that we have looked at the tip of the iceberg with these four vehicles.

> **The key to recognize here is that there are many ways to build wealth. You have a choice. Get educated and do it!**

All we are doing is playing with numbers to create spreads. This is what you need to know as a wealth builder: It's a financing game. It's not about real estate. It's not about private lending. It's not about life insurance policies. It's not about businesses.

It's about financing.

> **The main lesson of this book is that wealth is nothing but a financing game!**

Wealth as a financing game was the main lesson my mentor began to teach me the day we ate lunch together at Chili's. There were follow-up talks and question-and answer-periods. And along the way, other mentors have shared their knowledge and directed my motivation for creating wealth.

You, too, can build wealth, as long as you understand leverage and financing. In this book I've introduced you to that information.

I used to see 95% of real estate investors wasting their time on a "job." I hope you now understand that you don't need to look for another job in real estate. In fact, you never again need to waste your time on a job.

> **I hope you recognize how much you have learned already. The right education is the key to building wealth!**

"This is amazing! I didn't realize you could create arbitrage from so many things! Which one do you prefer?" I asked my mentor.

"It depends what you focus on. You can become an expert with one vehicle. You can expand to more. I use income properties and insurance arbitrage. Some of my wealthy friends use businesses. Others use private lending. They're all wealthy. It depends on your interests. But keep in mind that the vehicle doesn't matter much, as long as you understand that it's a financing game. The reason you focus on one or two vehicles," he continued, *"is so that you can then manage the risk better by understanding the risk factors."*

CHAPTER SUMMARY

- Here are a few vehicles we discussed:

  Vehicle One — Income Properties

  Vehicle Two — Private Lending

  Vehicle Three — Insurance Arbitrage

  Vehicle Four — Low-Tech Businesses

- The key to recognize here is that there are many ways to build wealth. You have a choice. Get educated and do it!

- It's not about real estate. It's not about private lending. It's not about life insurance policies. It's not about businesses. It's about financing.

- I hope you recognize how much you have learned already. The right education is the key to building wealth!

PART THREE

The Appreciation Column

CHAPTER THIRTEEN

The Appreciation Column

"We've talked about the middle column, the Cash Flow column, in some detail now. What about the left-hand column — the Appreciation column? Tell me more about that."

My mentor's computer interrupted the flow of the conversation with a ding. He had received an e-mail or a reminder. He turned to his computer and said, with a smile, "Wouldn't it have been great if you had bought Microsoft stock when it first came out?" He clicked on the mouse and typed something on his computer keyboard. "Okay, appreciation," he said, turning to me. "Are you sure you really want to know all this?" he chuckled.

WE'VE CONSIDERED THE APPRECIATION COLUMN AND HOW TO TURN IT into cash flow.

Actually, it's more appropriate to define "appreciation," as used here, as appreciating assets that generate equity for you.

APPRECIATION	CASH FLOW	CASH INFLUX
• Forced Appreciation • Timing Market • Normal Market • SFR in Appreciating Market • **NEGATIVE Cash Flow**	• Income Properties • Paper • Businesses	• Flipping • Foreclosure • Rehab • Wholesale
GOAL: *Build equity to turn into cash flow*	GOAL: *Passive income > expenses*	GOAL: *Fund appreciation and cash flow deals*
RICH	WEALTHY	JOB

FIGURE 63: The Appreciation Column

Now, remember that equity, in and of itself, does nothing for you. You can't eat it. You can't buy food with it. It only makes your net worth look good on paper. You "grow" this equity to either swap into cash or to move into the Cash Flow column.

When transferring equity from the Appreciation column into cash flow, you can assume you'll get between 10% and 12% return for the equity transferred over. That can mean that $1 million of equity can generate between $100,000 and $120,000 per year in cash flow if you buy correctly.

So think of the Appreciation column as *future* cash flow. You raise this equity for several years and then end up transferring it into the middle column (Cash Flow) to generate cash flow. You do so by something called a "1031 exchange." A 1031 tax-deferred exchange is one of the best gifts the government has given us. The tax on the gain of a property is deferred until some future date (as long as we buy another property).

Goal of Appreciation Column

Notice in the figure above that the goal of the Appreciation column is to "Build equity to turn into cash flow." It is also labeled "Rich." One who is rich is currently defined as an individual with a net worth of at least 1 million U.S. dollars or who has made at least $200,000 each year for the past two years ($300,000 with his or her spouse if married) and have the expectation of making the same amount this year.

This is also the definition of an "accredited investor."

As I explained early in this book, the problem with the Appreciation column is that many people strive to be rich before becoming wealthy. That results in a high net worth without the passive income coming in. Typically, doctors are rich, for example. The problem is that if they lose their job, their entire livelihood is threatened. It's not unusual for people in similar positions to lose everything. They never had cash flow coming in. Net worth does not pay the bills; cash flow does.

I personally know of a man who was rich (on paper) because of the combined equity of well over $1 million in 10 properties he owned. However, he had no passive income. He eventually lost his job, all of his savings (having to pay for all the negative cash flow), and his 10 properties, including his primary home. Sadly, his wife could not cope with being homeless and having to live with her parents, so the family separated. She left her husband and took the kids! Wanting to be rich, they were too focused on the left-hand column. They never understood that they had to become wealthy before becoming rich.

Building equity is just a means to get you to the cash flow in the future. The sooner you turn the equity into cash flow, the better.

Building Equity Fast

Most people think that building equity takes a long time. You have to buy an asset and wait for its value to appreciate over time, which could take forever. However, there are strategies for wealth builders to choose that will speed up the process.

- Build immediate equity by buying assets under market value. For example, buying a $400,000 single-family residence for $320,000, earns — immediately — $80,000 in equity. Then turn the equity into cash flow.

- Pay down the mortgage on investment properties, but without additional payments. Use leverage and the Debt Management System (see Resources section for more information). You can pay down the mortgage in one-half to one-third the time without making additional interest payments. Everyone should be doing this!
- Time the market. Buy when everyone else is selling. This is probably the best time to buy, but the hardest for people to do. The richest investors "buy when there is blood on the streets." They are known as contrarian investors.
- Use leverage to maximize equity. We covered this in detail in Chapter 6.
- Buy the right property type. Single-family residences appreciate faster and better than condos. Condos appreciate last in a good market and drop first in a bad market. Also, avoid high-end homes. Stick to single-family homes in good neighborhoods for best appreciation.
- Buy in traditionally appreciating markets. In California appreciation over the past 25 years has maintained a steady 8%; nationwide, average appreciation for single-family residences is just under 6%. In California, $10,000,000 worth of single-family residences will average $800k in equity per year.

Following are some more-advanced methods for experienced investors. Some of these are covered in more detail in ~~The Wealthy Code Inner Circle~~. MPact Wealth trainings (Refer to the Resources section.)

- Buy with seller financing. This is best for building appreciation with 0% or low-interest financing. Some 30% of America has fully paid homes. This allows for seller financing.
- Equity Share. This is an advanced strategy. Buy a portion of a property. Be the down payment partner, and let your partner carry the mortgage, or vice versa.
- Straight options. Real estate options are the fastest way to build equity and cover the downside; option a property and "1031" the option without "owning" the building. This method makes it possible to build six-figure equity fast; however, it is an advanced strategy.

- Lease options. Lease option the property by tying it up at today's price and for an extended time frame. Use future equity to buy cash flow properties.

Fast Equity Example

Buy a single-family residence, priced under market in an appreciating market, and use Debt Management System to pay it down. Consider this: in the San Francisco Bay Area you can buy a home worth $800,000 for $700,000. In four or five years it might be worth $1 million, you've paid down the mortgage, and you have $650,000 worth of equity that you can transfer via a 1031 exchange from the left column (Appreciation) to the center column (Cash Flow) to give you $78,000 per year from just one property. Imagine having a whole bunch of properties that fit the same criteria.

"It's interesting that you say to use single-family homes for building equity fast and not for cash flow. Many experts out there talk about buying them for rental properties. You say not to use single-family homes for cash flow, but more for building equity. You then use that equity to buy income properties such as apartment buildings," I observed.

"Well, single-family homes might provide cash flow in certain areas," my mentor acknowledged, "but they are actually bad cash flow vehicles. If they do provide cash flow, that's fine, but you should buy them as an equity-building strategy. Do you have any rental properties for cash flow now?"

"Yes, quite a few," I boasted. "In fact, I have them all over the United States. I just bought some in Rochester, New York, for cash...."

"Sell them," he interrupted. "Sell them."

"Why? They're cash-flowing $400 per month per duplex!"

"Sell them" he interrupted again, laughing. "Donald Trump says, 'If you're going to think, you might as well think big!' Sell them."

I didn't. I kept them. Eighteen months later, I learned my lesson. He was right. I ended up selling them.

CHAPTER SUMMARY

- Appreciation column is to grow equity and turn it into cash or cash flow.
- To turn equity into cash flow, move the equity from the Appreciation column to the Cash Flow column. Typically, you do this through the sale of the asset and the use of 1031 exchange into the purchase of another asset in the middle column.
- There are strategies that allow you to build equity fast. You don't have to wait for appreciation alone.

CHAPTER FOURTEEN

Wealth Farmer

"What are those labels?" I asked my mentor as we took a stretch break from all this overwhelming information. I was pointing to three framed pictures of what looked like labels found on food jars.

"Oh, those are my dad's. He was a farmer. They were some of the first labels he used in his business."

"What did he farm?" I asked.

"Mostly fruits."

"In a way, we're all farmers," I said. "You farm for money, though."

Farming Your Cash Flow Crops

YOU MUST THINK OF YOURSELF AS A FARMER — A WEALTH FARMER! Just as a farmer plants different crops (e.g., pears, apples, grapes, and oranges) in his fields, there are "wealth pairs" and "equity pairs" in your fields (portfolio).

Wealth pairs generate cash flow; equity pairs generate equity.

Each wealth pair consists of two things: leverage and the income-producing asset, where the asset generates more than the financing costs — i.e., positive leverage.

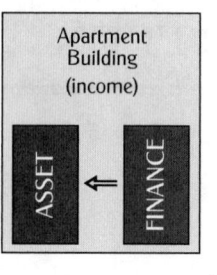
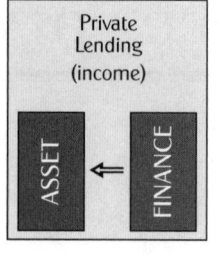
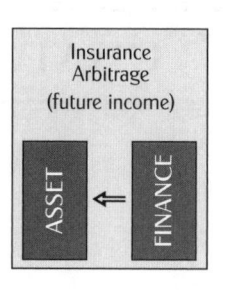

FIGURE 64: Wealth Pairs

A wealth pair could be an apartment building and the leverage that goes along with it to create a spread, generating cash flow into your pocket. Below is an expanded view of what you would find in a wealth pair.

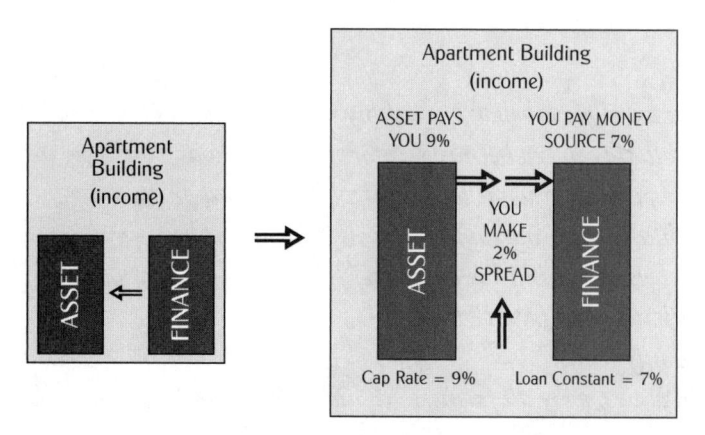

FIGURE 65: Wealth Pair Expanded (Example)

A wealth pair could also be a private lending deal and the leverage that goes with it to put that income stream from the spread into your pocket. It could be the insurance arbitrage (future income) I described earlier, using an asset to put the money into your pocket in the future. It could be any of those.

Ultimately, you will end up with many wealth pairs. Your portfolio of wealth pairs might look like Figure 66.

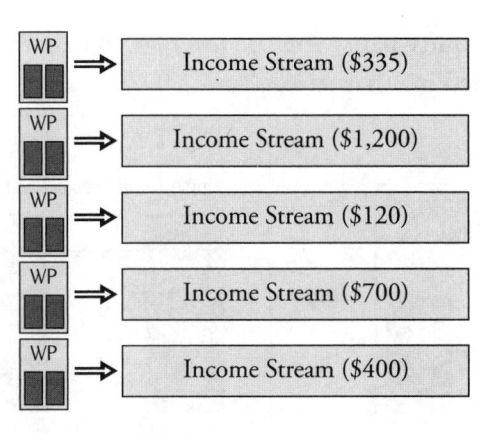

FIGURE 66: Wealth Pair Streams of Income

The "WP" in the diagram above stands for "wealth pair." Each pair generates an income stream. For some, the income stream will be consistent, others will increase over time, while still others will diminish over time. As a wealth farmer you have to keep growing those wealth pairs.

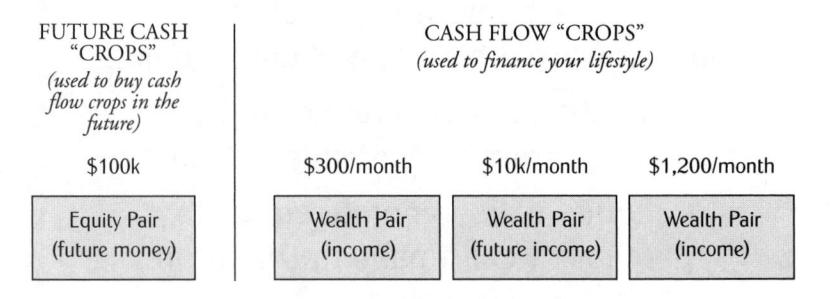

FIGURE 67: Wealth Farmer with Wealth and Equity Pairs

On the right-hand side of the figure above, notice the wealth pairs. These are pumping cash flow to you every month. You just have to manage the risk and maintain your portfolio of wealth pairs.

On the left-hand side of the figure above, notice that we have future cash crops. These are not income-producing crops yet. They grow equity for you that can be used to buy wealth pairs in the future for cash flow.

These are your equity pairs. You use leverage to maximize the appreciation, as explained in Chapter 6.

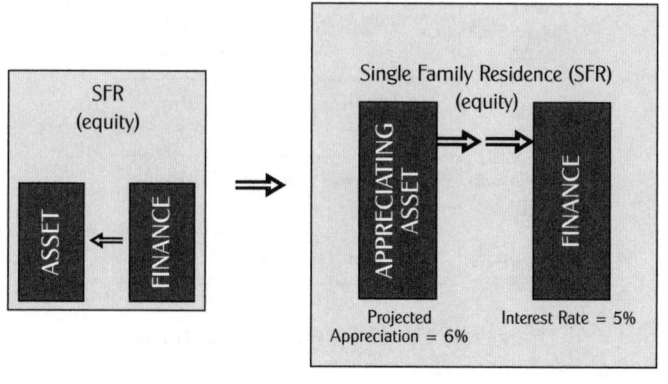

FIGURE 68: Equity Pair Expanded (Example)

Above is an expanded view of what you would find in an equity pair.

> ## As a wealth farmer,
> ## you grow wealth pairs and equity pairs.
> ### Wealth pairs generate cash flow
> ### from the spreads.
> ### Equity pairs generate equity to
> ### purchase wealth pairs in the future.

So as a farmer, you're always growing wealth pairs for cash flow and equity pairs for equity that will eventually buy you more wealth pairs.

Here's what your portfolio might look like.

APPRECIATION	CASH FLOW	CASH INFLUX
1031 EXCHANGES *You are "growing" these to turn them into streams of income.*		• Flipping • Foreclosure • Rehab • Wholesale
SFR — shared equity	Income property 2	
SFR — forced appreciation	Business	
SFR — in app. market	Income property 1	
	Secured Note 1	
GOAL: *Build equity to turn into cash flow*	GOAL: *Passive income > expenses*	GOAL: *Fund appreciation and cash flow deal*
RICH	**WEALTHY**	**JOB**

FIGURE 69: Wealth Farmer Portfolio
(SFR =Single-family residence)

In the left-hand column, you're building equity (equity pairs) to reinvest in the middle column for cash flow. Equity pairs are appreciating assets. You move them into the center column for additional cash flow. You might consider doing this with 1031 exchanges.

Just think of the assets under the Appreciation column as the crops you're growing so you can use them to buy more seeds to plant into the Cash Flow column.

"So do you know what your name, 'George,' means?" asked my mentor, showing a mischievous smile.

"No," I replied, wondering where this was leading.

"Farmer," he laughed.

CHAPTER SUMMARY

- As a wealth farmer, you grow wealth pairs and equity pairs.
- Wealth pairs generate cash flow from the spreads.
- Equity pairs generate equity to purchase wealth pairs in the future.
- As a wealth farmer, you're always looking at your portfolio of crops — both wealth pairs and equity pairs.

PART FOUR

Conclusion

CHAPTER FIFTEEN

Conclusion

"Wow! This is a lot of information!"

"Before long it will be second nature to you!" my mentor assured me. "It's like riding a bicycle. Before long, you don't even have to think about it. The unfortunate thing is that many people don't know that this information is the foundation to wealth. There's a lot more, of course, but every investor needs to know this much before doing anything."

"My brain is fried! This is truly eye opening. Can we continue tomorrow?" I asked.

"Let's do it next week, Farmer George."

CONGRATULATIONS.

YOU NOW HAVE THE FOUNDATION TO BECOMING WEALTHY.

The Wealthy Code boils down to a financing game. It's not about real estate. It's not about the stock market. It's none of that. It's purely a financing game. Find an asset that generates cash flow; find a way to borrow against it using positive leverage; identify the volatility of the income and manage that risk; and, finally, structure the right down payment. Then move on to the next deal.

If you understand that, then you understand what it takes to build wealth and, equally important, what you need to do to stop wasting your time and money buying things you don't need.

Unfortunately, many people have become programmed that leverage (the use of debt) is bad. However, as you have read in Robert Kiyosaki's books, and in this book, the use of debt plays a critical role in becoming wealthy. Kiyosaki refers to "bad debt" and "good debt" (i.e., positive leverage, neutral leverage, and negative leverage). However in all cases, there is one thing evident. You have to become comfortable using debt to become wealthy.

You can choose to "save" money for the rest of your life to achieve any measurable wealth, or you can learn to use leverage — understand it, measure it, manage it, and ultimately use it to become wealthy much faster.

Resources to Use

Feel free to download and use the tools available for some of the calculations I have covered in this book. The Resources section (page 159) contains all the links you need.

Also in the Resources section, you'll find some great vehicles for using leverage. At our classes I go into a lot more detail and show students how to further analyze data. I also give students more-advanced calculators to help them really make the most of their time and education. I want them to have all the tools and knowledge to make great decisions and get out there and amass the wealth they deserve.

For those of you interested in continuing your pursuit of wealth, you're welcome to become part of a community of individuals with the same goals. As a member of *The Wealthy Code Inner Circle*, you get access to more training, resources, invitations to live events, and monthly newsletters. For more information and a 30-day trial, refer to the Resources section.

Many people ask me where to start. As my mentor told me, that's your decision to make. But I can tell you my favorite thing — being a private lender without using my own money or credit. Private lending is one of the most amazing leveraging opportunities out there. You can find more information on private lending in the Resources section.

In conclusion, Robert Kiyosaki opened our eyes to the best, most useful definition of the word "wealth." In this book, I explained what it takes to control wealth, to measure wealth, to build wealth, and ultimately, to become truly wealthy. The information my mentor passed along to me as a gift has changed my life, so I pass it on to you hoping that you can initiate changes in your own financial life.

I can tell you one thing with certainty: In the future you will look back and say, "I wish I had done it" or "I'm glad I did it." Whichever path you choose is up to you, but you now have all the information you need to be able to start to build wealth for yourself. I've given you the Wealthy Code.

May our paths one day cross!

Today, I turned on the television. There was nothing exciting to watch . . . again! So I started channel surfing. One show piqued my interest.

Sound familiar? This time, my entire family was watching with me: my wife Clara, my son Emile, my two daughters Amanda and Christine, and my mother Jacqueline.

The show was "Shark Tank." And so began a whole new chapter in my life. . . .

On Monday morning, I walked into my mentor's office. Our conversation began with the next set of lessons on . . . The Bankers Code. This blew my mind.

Resources

Visit www.mpactwealth.com/TWCBook
To access the following resources.

Tools and Software

The Simple Financial Leverage Calculator

Download this for free (along with some other calculators) at
www.TheWealthyCodeTools.com

Cost of Money Calculator

~~Available for purchase at~~ **www.WealthClasses.com/cost_software**

Debt Management System

like George describes in the book

~~If you want to~~ find out if you qualify to pay off your mortgage fast, using
the "flow of money" ~~in your life, visit~~ **www.DebtFreeSecret.com**. Not
everyone qualifies for this program, but those that *who can* do are paying down
their debt in 1/3 the time. When you visit **www.DebtFreeSecret.com** *this page*
you will register to watch a free training video. *and then* After that you ~~will be~~ *can*
~~able to~~ schedule a complimentary one-on-one ~~strategy session on how~~
~~you can begin getting debt free!~~ *meeting to see if this will work for you.*

159

Further Education

The Wealthy Code Inner Circle

Become part of *The Wealthy Code Inner Circle*. This is a community of individuals looking to build wealth. Receive access to more online training and other resources to help you achieve your financial goals. Receive a 30-day membership trial for $1. Visit **www.TheWealthyCode.com/dollar** and use the coupon code "Book" (without quotation marks).

Private Lending Mastery

In this home study course (you can also register for the *live* training), you learn to make money like banks do. You learn to use leverage and arbitrage to generate cash flow — just like the banks — secured by real collateral. **www.TheBankersCode.com**

Apartment Investing Mastery

In this home study course (you can also register for the *live* training), you learn to generate cash flow as an apartment-building owner. You learn to use leverage and arbitrage to generate cash flow just like the very wealthy — from apartment buildings. **www.ApartmentInvestingMastery.com**

Further Free Education

The Wealthy Code Seminar

Join George Antone for more training taking the information from this book to a whole new level. Learn advanced secrets every savvy wealth builder should know and cannot afford to ignore. Simply visit **www.TheWealthyCodeSeminar.com** and enter the code: WEALTHYNOW to gain free access.

Complimentary 30-Minute Strategy Session

You receive a 30-minute "Wealth Building" strategy session with the purchase of this book! Contact us at: (888) 888-3612 or **www.30MinuteStrategy.com** and ask for your complimentary strategy session to get to the next level in your wealth plans today.

Complimentary Sneak Peek

Get a sneak peek into the upcoming book, *The Bankers Code*. Visit **www.TheBankersCodeBook.com** today.

Reference #:_____

Contact Information

Company: WealthClasses LLC
Toll-free phone: (888) 888-3612
Web: www.WealthClasses.com
E-mail: TheWealthyCodeBook@wealthclasses.com

TWCSupport@MPactWealth.com

INDEX